Social
Traps

by John G. Cross and Melvin J. Guyer

Ann Arbor
The University of Michigan Press

1983   1982   1981   1980   5   4   3   2

Library of Congress Cataloging in Publication Data

Cross, John G
  Social traps.

  Bibliography: p.
  1. Human behavior.   2.   Choice (Psychology)
3.   Social problems.   4.   Learning, Psychology of.
5.   Social legislation—United States.   I.   Guyer,
Melvin J., joint author.
HM251.C93   301.1   79–26392
ISBN 0–472–06315–4

Illustrations, in order of appearance, are reproduced through the courtesy of
the following collections:

The Fall, by Rembrandt van Rijn (Rijksmuseum, The Hague)
Knight, Death and the Devil, by Albrecht Dürer (Kupferstichdakinett, Berlin)
Death and the Young Man, by the Housebook Master (Rijksmuseum,
  Amsterdam)
A Rake's Progress, Plate III, by William Hogarth (The University of Michigan
  Museum of Art, gift of Jean Paul Slusser)
Four Horsemen of the Apocalypse, by Albrecht Dürer (Trustees of the British
  Museum, London)
Le Mauvaise Côté des Nouveaux Omnibus, by Honoré Daumier (private
  collection)
Civil War, by George Grosz (Donald Morris Gallery, Detroit)
Grand Escalier du Palais de Justice, by Honoré Daumier (private collection)

Dedicated to the memories of
Pearl Guyer and Roderic M. Cross

Preface

Rational people indulge innumerable silly habits, and while some of these, like refusing to walk under ladders and voting straight party tickets, are relatively innocuous, others, like consuming hard drugs or overusing chemical pesticides, present massive challenges to contemporary society. Concerned by such apparent contradictions between common sense and common behavior and finding a joint interest in the possibility that contemporary theories of behavior change might shed some light upon these problems, a group of four researchers in the Mental Health Research Institute of the University of Michigan established a series of semiformal seminars where the contrasts between decision-theoretic models of rational behavior and psychological theories of learning could be discussed. This book is in the nature of a summary of those discussions. The theory presented here cannot be regarded as a fully developed or even wholly consistent one. The range of problems which seemed to be amenable to our analysis is far too broad to be encompassed by any group of four persons, however diverse their interests. Indeed, many of the views described in the following pages are not even held unanimously, although there is agreement upon the essential structure of our model and how it is to be used.

In writing the book, it became obvious very soon that a four-authored work would be a practical impossibility, and perhaps only because we happened to be the first to compile a complete draft, we found ourselves with the entire responsibility. This is embarrassing to us, not only because the substance of the work is by no means all our own, but also because the restricted authorship has limited the range of perspectives that could be brought to bear upon the problem as a whole. In this regard, John Cross makes use of his background as an economist but denies that he can speak with any authority upon the psychological elements which play such an important part in our over-all conception. On the other hand, Melvin Guyer, as a social psychologist and attorney, has a background which includes a large number of laboratory studies of human behavior. His knowledge of experimental "prisoner's dilemma" games pro-vides much of the underlying material found in chapter 7, and chapter 8, which discusses legal devices and their possible con-tribution to the resolution of traps, reflects his association with the legal profession.

The other two contributors in this research were Professors Gardner Quarton and John Platt. Platt's belief—that the princi-ples of operant conditioning are essential to the understanding of human behavior—gave our work its orientation toward learning theory. Moreover, his interest in resource conserva-tion, growth/no-growth controversies, and problems of urban civilization provided the subject matter for many of our semi-nars. Although he has been unable to make any direct contri-bution to this book, he has presented some written material in the August, 1973, issue of the *American Psychologist*.

We also deeply regret that administrative time pressures prevented Dr. Gardner Quarton from taking part. It was he who provided the psychological orientation for many of our discussions as well as the selection of the title of this book. Moreover, his sympathetic view of social problems as "traps" or even "illnesses" (perhaps attributable to his background as a psychiatrist) rather than as the handiwork of conscienceless people brought a positive tone to all of our discussions.

Thanks are due finally to the Mental Health Research Insti-tute, whose support made this research possible and whose staff has provided invaluable typing, organizational, and gen-eral support services throughout the project. We are particu-larly grateful to Adele Henry for her great patience and excel-lent work in the face of what must have seemed an unending series of revisions and retypings of an already overworked manuscript.

John Cross
Melvin Guyer

Contents

1 *Introduction*

The Fall

Rembrandt van Rijn
etching 1638

In the eyes of the ancients, the apple was the first trap ever set for humanity. The knowledge of evil and all its penalties came only after a foolish indulgence.

Some time ago a specialist in international relations at the University of Michigan addressed a seminar on the subject of diplomatic decision making. During his talk, he described his personal impressions of the people who make important foreign policy decisions in most major nations of the world. His characterizations were overwhelmingly complimentary, and they included such virtues as experience, intelligence, competence, and sometimes even a genuine concern for the peace, security, and overall well-being of the inhabitants of the world at large. How then, he asked, is it possible for these qualified and well-intentioned persons to make decisions that reduce and sometimes even destroy the peace, security, and well-being of the very populations they are supposed to represent? He saw the situation as a kind of international social pathology in which leaders seem to be drawn inexorably, through their own choices, to precisely the consequences they appear anxious to avoid.

Having no satisfactory explanation for this phenomenon, the speaker, like so many other liberal foreign policy observers, forced himself to the conclusion that national leaders are not so intelligent or well-intentioned as he had thought them to be. His originally complimentary impressions degenerated into suggestions that in fact their experience must have served only to generate a series of unsupportable myths about the behavior of other nations, that they must be unable to distinguish their own public-relations pronouncements from international reality, and that they must have become so chauvinistic in outlook that they are more likely to believe what they read in their own domestic newspapers than what they learn at the conference table.

The view that international conflict results from the incompetence and chauvinism of policy makers is, in many respects, very seductive. It provides what appears to be a straightforward and immediate solution to the problem: one must simply remove the people who are making wrong foreign policy decisions and replace them with individuals who are more qualified and who possess more cosmopolitan outlooks. But the more things change, the more they stay the same and, in the view of most observers, even enlightened new appointees quickly adjust to their circumstances and soon are found carrying out policies essentially equivalent to those for which they had condemned their predecessors. The attitude that blame for serious social problems can be laid at the feet of a few identifiable, incompetent, or amoral individuals is not confined to the international sphere. Thus, the conventional view would have us blame drug consumption on the dope pushers, would have us punishing the steel industry for polluting the atmosphere, and would have us holding the tobacco companies responsible for lung cancer.

A competing view that seems to be equally simpleminded attributes a wide variety of social problems to ignorance and a lack of education. If only people knew what the consequences of their behavior would be, this argument goes, they would change their ways. In our high schools we have seen a proliferation of "drug education" programs designed to combat the drug problem, and we have generated extensive publicity about the dire consequences of smoking, requiring that warning messages be printed on packets of cigarettes in hopes that this will reduce consumption. During the 1960s, many social scientists held the opinion that if we could simply teach foreign policy decision makers how things really are, they might change their policies and perhaps even bring about a world peace. Evidence, however, does not support their naive notions. Studies now indicate that drug education courses may actually increase drug experimentation, cigarette consumption continues to rise despite the warnings, and foreign affairs experts surely ought to know enough history to be able to forecast the likely consequences of constant confrontation. It is surprising that the popular faith in simple education can be so persistent in the face of repeated demonstrations that it may not be effective at all.

The central thesis of this book is that a wide variety of recognized social problems can be regarded from a third point of view. Drug use, air pollution, and international conflict are all instances of what we have called "social traps." Put simply, a social trap is a situation characterized by multiple but conflicting rewards. Just as an ordinary trap entices its prey with the offer of an attractive bait and then punishes it by capture, so the social situations which we include under the rubric "social traps" draw their victims into certain patterns of behavior with promises of immediate rewards and then confront them with consequences that the victims would rather avoid. On the level of the individual person, examples are easy to think of. In the case of smoking (accepting the proposition that cigarette smoking causes a variety of illnesses), we find the cigarette smoker enjoying at first the repeated gratification of smoking, and only after a long delay, when it is much too late, does he find himself faced with the disagreeable consequences. Of course it is easy to take one of the conventional views of the smoker's problem: accuse him of lack of willpower, ignorance, or stupidity; assert that he simply does not care now what the consequences may be later on; or even argue that he willingly and knowingly accepted the risk of a shortened life as a reasonable price for the pleasure of smoking. These we take to be not only extremely unsympathetic, but also hopelessly naive attitudes. The pleasures associated with smoking have a physical presence and immediacy that is entirely absent in the case of its other consequences. Moreover, any avoidance which might be induced through threats of future punishment is further reduced by the fact that the punishment by no means occurs with certainty, making it possible for the smoker to avoid even the anticipation of pain with the rationalization that that sort of thing only happens to other people. In addition, the connection between cigarette smoking and lung cancer or heart disease has been established only at a fairly abstract intellectual level—that is, through statistical and other suggestive scientific evidence, not through direct or immediate observation. Thus, whereas the cause-effect relationship between the cigarette and its immediate rewards are obvious to the smoker, the cause-effect relationships between the cigarette and its consequent diseases is not: a purely intellectual understanding of this second linkage is no match for the direct physical relation which characterizes the first.

Imputations of ignorance, foolishness, or a weak moral character may convince some as appropriate explanations for a few traps such as drug abuse, smoking, or even international conflict; nevertheless, there exist many situations which conform to our definition of a trap that cannot be approached from this perspective at all. An example is the 5:00 P.M. traffic jam that arises as commuters try all at the same time to go home from their urban workplaces. One cannot reasonably argue that everyone caught in such a jam has made a mistake out of ignorance. The traffic snarl arises every workday afternoon at the same time and is an ordinary experience for every commuter. Moreover, the jam is clearly a collective problem. From the point of view of each commuter, the jam is not his personal responsibility; it can be expected to occur at the usual time whatever he chooses to do as an individual, and all he can do if he wishes to avoid it is leave for home an hour and a half later than everyone else. If this alternative is not attractive to him, he will brave the traffic along with the others.

Nevertheless, the existing situation is surely not all for the best; there must be a more efficient way to move people without causing hundreds of commuters to curse their fellow man and burn scarce gallons of gasoline as they try to get home to dinner. Public transportation may conserve fuel, but even this alternative is subject to the same crushing rush-hour problem. As many people have suggested, however, if one could only stagger the times at which offices open and close so that some commuters could start out at four o'clock, some at five, and some at six (instead of all together at five), there would not be any jam, whatever the means of transportation. Nevertheless, despite the fact that every commuter understands this and every city government understands it, the necessary coordination of schedules has rarely come about. The point of our example is that unless some traffic controller assumes dictatorial powers, such collective coordination is not possible. There is not sufficient incentive for any individual commuter to leave his workplace at a time other than the prevailing closing time, and that being the case, noboby leaves at any time other than five. Therefore, the aggregation of these fully informed individual decisions has led the entire society into a trap.

The Genesis of This Book

The notion of a social trap first arose during a series of seminars at the University of Michigan Mental Health Research Institute. Discussions were focused upon the relevance of psychological learning theory for understanding social behavior and the potential application of learning theory to the modification of undesirable social behavior. We were impressed by the fact that practical applications of learning principles to behavior change ("behavior modification" as it has come to be known in many circles) have now become quite widespread, finding effective uses in all sorts of areas, ranging from the classroom to psychological therapy and even to correctional institutions. The potential which these psychological techniques have for altering human behavior is staggering, often raising frightening social and ethical issues. Our own concern was not primarily with behavior modification itself, however, but with the possibility that the same principles of learning might help to explain some apparent peculiarities in behavior that develop under uncontrolled, day-to-day circumstances. Many examples of human actions exist that are inconsistent with rationality or even with simple common sense, and the topics of our discussions turned more and more to the investigation of conditions under which ordinary learning processes could lead to seemingly pathological results.

The learning principles that seemed to bear the most fruit in this respect are related to the phenomenon known as *instrumental conditioning*, the process whereby systems of reward and punishment are thought to establish repetitive patterns of behavior. We recognized that ideally we should take a much broader view, and that it would be desirable to investigate viewpoints not relying so heavily upon mechanistic learning. In particular, more consideration of recently developed cognitive theories of learning might be appropriate. Unfortunately, it proves to be extraordinarily difficult to make the exogenous variables found in cognitive theories endogenous to the environmental circumstances that give rise to traps. At the present state of development, the application of cognitive theories to pragmatic ends would require the introduction of a whole range of personality variables that would not easily generalize into a predictive model. A narrower scope was inevitable, therefore, given the contemporary state of the art. The application of the principles of instrumental conditioning to practical problems is made easy by the relatively advanced state of the theory; also, to supplement the theory, there now exists a vast accumulation of experimental and practical evidence concerning both the development of habits and the nature of avoidance behavior. In the course of these experiments, a number of specific factors have been identified that influence the intensity and persistence of conditioned behavior; in fact, many of the factors have already been recognized by psychologists to be possible explanations for apparent deviations from strict rationality.

Although paradoxical behavior is uncovered during many learning experiments, we found that the general problem of deviations from rationality has never been investigated systematically. It may be that the use of experimental results in interpreting real-world behavior takes one far outside the controlled conditions under which the experiments were conducted. Many experimental psychologists are extremely reluctant to make extrapolations beyond the laboratory and refuse (at least in public) to draw any inferences from their discoveries that might be applied outside the experimental environment. It is argued that what one learns from an experiment is how a subject may behave in that experiment, and very little more. While this stance may reflect a laudable scientific conservatism, it is at the same time almost completely useless. Not only does it inhibit the generalization of the science, but it may even prevent many knowledgeable researchers from participating in the practical applications of their own findings. There is danger, certainly, in drawing real-world inferences from laboratory results, but we feel the best way to minimize the danger and still retain a useful theory is not to refuse to make any such inferences at all, but to restrict ourselves to only the most general and widely confirmed of laboratory findings. We are confident that all of the properties of learning that are central to our discussions are quite general and arise with great regularity.

A second obstacle to our analysis of nonrational learned behavior was that the conditions under which it may arise are a bit more complicated than those usually constructed. As a matter of fact, most of the literature on instrumental conditioning and all of its practical applications to behavior modification are confined to unidimensional situations in which the behavior to be learned is inevitably rational under the circumstances. The subject in an experiment may be rewarded if he behaves in a certain way, with the sensible result that he repeats the behavior; or, an activity previously rewarded may later be followed by the absence of reward or by a punishment, with the sensible results that the habit is extinguished. Such simple, single-valued situations must be constructed if one is to acquire some understanding of the dynamics of the learning mechanism, but they by no means correspond to real-life circumstances. Most decisions that we ordinarily make require that we select our behavior from a variety of possible alternatives, each of which may produce both rewards and punishments simultaneously. The customer at the meat counter of a supermarket must choose among chicken, fish, steak, frankfurters, pork roasts, hamburger, and lamb chops—each of which may produce an anticipatory salivation at the thought of consumption at dinner time. Today, however, the rewards of providing food for the table are accompanied by severely punishing prices. The wide range of choices, each accompanied by some combination of reward and punishment, constitutes a much more complicated situation than is described in most of the literature on learning.

Many psychologists appear to believe that these more general decision problems can be described in terms of simple extensions of one- or two-dimensional learning models. In many cases we would agree, but even elementary learning phenomena, when applied to some multiple-valued situations, will lead to quite unexpected outcomes. Cases which from a purely rationalistic point of view appear to lead to unreasonable and even dangerous behavior provide the subject matter for the chapters to follow.

Background Notes

There are a number of competing variations on the basic theories of instrumental conditioning, and it is our desire to avoid taking a position that implies strong support or rejection of any one or another of these theories. For the purposes of this book, there is no need to use more than the most elementary and generally accepted properties of learning; therefore, we shall confine ourselves to an outline of the meanings and uses of a few terms and concepts.

Contemporary theories of instrumental conditioning go well beyond E. L. Thorndike's early proposed simple connectionism (stimulus-response psychology), but they all reflect his so-called law of effect—the empirical principle which states that when any action is closely followed by a reward, that action is "reinforced," meaning simply that it is then more likely to recur in the future than it would have been without the reward. Commonplace applications of the principle range from the observation that a hungry pigeon, upon receiving food after pecking at a colored disk, is likely to peck at that disk again to the deliberate use of rewards (money, candy, or effusive praise) to encourage a child to repeat a superior performance in school. Since in such cases the likelihood of the rewarded action is increased, the term *positive reinforcement* is ordinarily applied.

In contrast to the carrot (reward), the function of the stick (punishment) is harder to describe, mainly because the role of punishment in shaping behavior is not universally accepted among psychologists themselves. In particular, punishment is rarely seen to operate symmetrically with rewards. Thus, if an action is punished, the future likelihood of that action is not necessarily reduced, and certainly it is not reduced by an amount comparable to the increase that a reward might engender. It is usually accepted, however, that the successful avoidance of a feared punishment is reinforcing. That is, if some behavior is seen to lead to punishment and some alternative behavior, otherwise comparable, successfully avoids that punishment, then the individual is more likely to choose the alternative in the future, just as though he had been rewarded. In some cases, the distinction between the avoidance of punishment and positive reinforcement is trivial (does one heat a house in order to be warm, or to avoid being cold?); nevertheless it will be useful to continue to distinguish situations that produce tangible rewards from those involving punishments. We may occasionally use the term *negative reinforcement* to refer to the process of reinforcement through successful avoidance of punishment, although this term is usually restricted to situations in which behavior reduces the severity of an existing state of unpleasantness.

Since we are concerned with the overall effectiveness of behavior, we cannot forget that the reward or threatened punishment that shapes future behavior also influences immediate welfare. The child who is rewarded with a piece of candy is, to that extent, better off—whatever the influence of the candy may be for future activity. The child who is punished is thereby harmed, and even if the future behavior shaped by that punishment is beneficial, the present harm must be weighed against the future benefits if the situation is to be evaluated properly.

The Nature of a Trap

Putting all this into a more colloquial framework, a reinforcer is both a simple reward, gratifying in its own right, and a sort of traffic signal which directs future behavior. If a guest tells an off-color story at a cocktail party and nobody laughs, he has in effect been given both disappointment and a red light which signals that his behavior is inappropriate and that he should avoid telling such stories in the future. If everyone laughs heartily and responds with stories of their own, he has, besides his gratification, a green light indicating that such behavior is accepted and will continue to be rewarding. With regard to future behavior, if one speaks loosely of a reward, one is speaking of a green light or something that will induce previous behavior to recur. When one speaks of a punishment, one is referring to a red light, something whose avoidance will reinforce alternative forms of behavior. In general, we will speak of reinforcers in these terms, referring to them as signals that direct individuals through a complex set of behavioral alternatives and lead, finally, to some sort of destination.

Reinforcement learning has traditionally been seen as a form of adaptation. By its means, animals can adjust to changes in the environment in a manner which facilitates survival. Reinforcing stimuli from the environment act so as to modify and select some behaviors over others; behaviors that produce or are associated with positively reinforcing events show an increased probability of occurring in similar situations in the future, and behaviors that produce or are associated with punishing events show a decreasing probability of occurring in subsequent similar situations. Under ordinary circumstances, this is a neat and effective device for getting along in a world that is much too complex to permit detailed planning. All that is required is that the stimuli which are positively reinforcing are also "good" for the organism in some sense, and that avoided events are also those which are "not good" for the organism. Usually this is just the way things work, and it is a good idea to stop doing whatever causes pain and to continue or repeat behaviors that have produced pleasant consequences.

Social traps represent situations in which our generally successful learning strategy leads us astray. The behavior that receives the green light becomes supplanted by or is accompanied by an unavoidable punishment. Again, cigarette smoking provides a simple example: the gratification associated with smoking encourages future behavior of the same kind, while the painful illness associated with that same behavior does not occur until a point very distant in the future; and when, finally, the illness does occur, no behavioral adjustments exist that are sufficient to avoid it.

Some traps are even recursive in that the reinforcements which establish them are actually increased by the fact that the victim is already in a trap. Thus the cigarette smoker may calm his anxiety over lung disease with another smoke. Examples of this sort of situation are surprisingly numerous. A morning hangover may be treated with a stiff drink ("the hair of the dog that bit me"). Gamblers frequently attempt to cover losses by playing long shots. A spendthrift may see new loans as the only means for covering old debts. A man whose dog refuses to return upon command may capture and beat the animal only to find him less obedient at the next command, requiring still sterner punishment.

In many cases, the aversive consequences of some behavior are imposed on persons other than the one receiving positive reinforcement. If a steel mill is polluting the atmosphere, it is not, by and large, the owners of the steel mills who are suffering from poisoned air, but the people who happen to live downwind. The commuter who drives his car home at five o'clock in the afternoon contributes to the severity of the traffic jam, thus affecting others who are also trying to get home at five o'clock. Many of the most frustrating social traps embody this symmetry in that when we follow what appear to be reasonable guides to our own behavior, we harm someone else, and when others follow what appear to be reasonable guides to them, they harm us.

All of these examples share a common feature—all involve individuals who use reinforcements like road signs, traveling in the direction of rewards and avoiding the paths marked by punishments. Generally, this is a good way for us to get where we would like to go. Occasionally, however, these road signs lead to unfortunate destinations. These are our social traps. Many of the traps to be discussed in this book are attributable to peculiar properties of the learning process itself. Research into the phenomenon of habit formation has uncovered a number of conditions that can lead to behavior which is at variance with the individual's own best interest or with the interest of society as a whole. While such conflicts are often quite obvious, it would be a great oversimplification to conclude that it is a mere failure to plan ahead that is responsible for social traps. Were we all possessed of ideal foresight, perfect self-control, and complete understanding of the intricate consequences of our behavior, then many (although still not all) social traps could be avoided. In fact, our decision-making capacities fall far short of these ideals, and we must rely upon experience under all but the simplest of circumstances. Moreover, as we shall see in later chapters, social traps often have the power not only to lead us into inferior modes of behavior, but also to influence our evaluations of the circumstances in which we find ourselves: to the victims of a trap, the existence of superior alternatives is often much less obvious than it is to those outside.

A second intention of this book is to show how the characterization of important social problems as traps can contribute to the development of effective "escapes." Most of our examples are widely recognized to be genuine social problems, but the inclination to look at them as unrelated phenomena has obscured the possibility that similar sorts of solutions may be available across the board. Furthermore, a redirection of emphasis toward the traplike character of these problems is intended to counter the temptation to treat our troubles as though they were the concoctions of ignorant or unethical individuals. Such attitudes lead inevitably to a lack of understanding of the problem and, worse, to a lack of sympathy or concern for the victims of traps. Our view of social traps as conflicting reinforcer situations has led us to believe that many of the solutions usually proposed for social problems will fail because they do not confront the actual forces which underlie the situations.

Thus the example of international conflict, with which we began this introduction, must be attributable to something other than ignorance: we all know that conflict is socially counterproductive, and yet that knowledge is not sufficient to stop it. Moreover, despite the common view that responsibility for conflict can be placed at the feet of a few identifiable national leaders, we have already noted that even the most enlightened replacement of foreign policy advisors has little effect on the policies that lead toward confrontation. In our view, the substitution of one individual for another does nothing to alter the fundamental reinforcement structure; therefore, whatever one's ideals may be, the learning process will direct behavior into the same channels. Similarly, because drug education has no fundamental impact upon the reinforcement potential of drugs, we would not expect it to influence drug use to any significant extent; since warnings on cigarette packages do not affect the physical pleasures of smoking, it is unlikely that they would achieve much success in inhibiting cigarette consumption. Warning messages and high school drug education courses can be defended only on an optimistic and, we believe, false premise: that people consciously direct their behavior toward what they intellectually know to be good for them, rather than permitting their behavior to be directed by the simpler and more immediate impacts of day-to-day rewards and punishments. Even those who are so fortunate as to possess the foresight and self-control requisite to optimal personal behavior are likely to find themselves the joint victims of traps that are set for their less fortunate contemporaries.

2

A Taxonomy of Traps

Knight, Death and the Devil

Albrecht Dürer
engraving 1513

The Christian knight of Dürer's engraving is not swayed by the enticements of the devil, nor is he afraid of the accomplice, Death, and we are left in little doubt as to the path which he intends to follow. Such a work was surely intended in part to serve as an inspiration to ordinary humans who, having less fortitude, are more readily drawn onto the easier behavioral paths.

Two roads diverged in a yellow wood,
And sorry I could not travel both
And be one traveler, long I stood
And looked down one as far as I could
To where it bent in the undergrowth;

Then took the other, as just as fair,
And having perhaps the better claim,
Because it was grassy and wanted wear;
Though as for that the passing there
Had worn them really about the same,

And both that morning equally lay
In leaves no step had trodden black
Oh, I kept the first for another day!
Yet knowing how way leads on to way,
I doubted if I should ever come back.

I shall be telling this with a sigh
Somewhere ages and ages hence:
Two roads diverged in a wood, and I—
I took the one less traveled by,
And that has made all the difference.
                    Robert Frost, "The Road Not Taken"

Most contemporary economic theory and much so-called decision theory presumes that each of us possesses a road map
from which we know, or at least can guess, to what destinations our behavior will take us. These theories then use the
properties of the destinations to predict the decision paths
rational people will follow. Learning theories suggest instead
that choices are made as we go along, that decisions are made
on the basis of relatively insignificant local details, and that
we only know the destinations after we have arrived. It is not
surprising that the behaviors predicted by these two models
can be quite different, or that once we know the destinations
and can reflect upon them, we might regret some of the
choices that led us to them.

Like their physical analogs, social traps are baited. The baits are the positive rewards which, through the mechanisms of learning, direct behavior along lines that seem right every step of the way but nevertheless end up at the wrong place. Complex patterns of reinforcement, motivation, and the structure of social situations can draw people into unpreferred modes of behavior, subjecting them to consequences that are not comprehended until it is too late to avoid them. Typical is the plight of the social drinker who, after the gaiety and freedom of a night's cocktail party, finds himself suffering the next morning's hangover and resolves, too late, to be more moderate in the future. In the morning, the scales tip clearly in favor of abstention. It is easy to resolve to be more temperate when there is no party in progress, but when the next occasion arises, the resolution is easily overcome and the trap reentered.

Another class of traps replaces Frost's grassy path with the traditionally unpleasant straight and narrow one. These are traps whose bait is unattractive or even noxious. Such traps might be called "negatively baited" and have their analog in the social traps which we term "countertraps." The physical version of a negatively baited trap is exemplified by animal drives where repellent stimuli, usually trappers themselves, push an animal or groups of animals into the entrance of the trap. Fans of old cowboy movies should be immediately reminded of the function of the box canyon used to capture just about everyone at some time or another. An example of a negatively baited trap is the fear of pain which leads us to avoid visits to the dentist's office. Although we have all been told that good preventive dental care requires two trips to the dentist's chair each year, few things are easier than semiannual forgetfulness. Avoiding the negative bait, we back into a trap, recognized only when those six-month visits begin to look good compared to the dental work their avoidance has necessitated.

Thus, in the ordinary trap, the bait draws the victim into behavior that ultimately leads to unhappy consequences, whereas in the countertrap, an aversive bait causes the victim to avoid a course of action which, if followed, would have brought about a preferred consequence. Strictly in terms of learning theory, there may be no real need to distinguish these two types of bait; the difference between positive and negative bait is technically the difference between positive and negative reinforcement. Nevertheless, we distinguish between traps and countertraps because their practical manifestations are often different. Countertraps (sins of omission) arise when we avoid potentially beneficial behavior, while traps (sins of commission) occur when we take potentially harmful courses of action.

It is no use to argue that rationalistic models are inconsistent with learning theory and, since learning models have by far the stronger experimental support, to reject rationality as a useful source of insight into human behavior. We believe that in most cases the learning mechanism is successful in directing us toward sensible goals, so that the two theories usually amount to the same thing. Our purpose here is to identify those special situations in which learning produces paths leading away from rationality, so that we know not only that inferior goals are being achieved, but in which directions the errors have been made.

We have isolated five separate types of circumstance in which reinforcer signals guide behavior to lead to inferior destinations. We have designated these situations as the five primary types of social traps, adding a sixth class that incorporates combinations of the other five. We do not pretend that these five primary traps are in any sense new to the social science literature. In fact, we have encountered previous discussions of most of the situations we use to define our traps, and in some cases the literature is very extensive. Our purpose is to demonstrate how a variety of deficiencies in behavior, some well understood and some not, can all be related to a single underlying process—the mechanism of reinforcement learning. Even those traps that have been investigated in the past have usually been developed independently of one another, and different traps have been approached as if they were entirely unrelated phenomena. Moreover, the generality of the procedures for escaping or avoiding traps is overlooked entirely. What we wish to stress in the following taxonomy, therefore, is the general perspective and unification of theory which an understanding of the learning process can bring to social problems.

Time-Delay Traps

It has been discovered from a variety of learning situations that substantial time lags between a behavior and an associated reinforcer will reduce drastically the power of the reinforcer to influence subsequent occurrences of the behavior. Indeed, in some animal experiments time lags of more than a few seconds appear to eliminate almost entirely the reinforcing effect of a reward. Human beings are able to bridge longer time gaps, although it is by no means a settled matter how long that gap may be. Neither are we certain of the mechanism that makes reinforcements effective over longer periods. Despite these unanswered questions, there is no doubt that a reduction in learning attributable to time delay affects all organisms more or less in the same way, and that lengthy time lags may prevent learning altogether. Thus, if one alternative action is followed by a delayed reward while another is followed by its reward almost immediately, it is the second that is likely to recur over and over, even though the first may provide a much more desirable outcome.

Instead of producing a tangible reward, the "rational" alternative may simply succeed in preventing a painful outcome that is contingent upon the trapped behavior but that occurs only after a time delay. The situation is nevertheless unchanged in principle. The immediately desirable consequence reinforces the wrong action, and since the undesirable consequence occurs only after a considerable lag, it has little effect on inhibiting a future recurrence of the same trap. Even though the same behavior may be repeated several times, its negative consequence may never be sufficiently contiguous to it to encourage selection of an alternative. This, for instance, is the predicament of our social drinker who repeatedly overindulges at parties despite any number of hangover-induced resolutions toward moderation. With respect to this example, it is interesting to speculate that the influence of the time lag appears to operate in both directions: overindulgence in alcohol seems less likely to occur immediately after a hangover (perhaps because the unpleasantness is still fresh in one's mind), and successful avoidance of the unpleasantness is a negative reinforcer that encourages the alternative behavior. It is only after the hangover has slipped into the past that the trap is set again, ready to be reentered.

If an action results in an immediate pleasant consequence followed only much later by an unpleasant consequence, the behavior and its immediate reward can be repeated several times before the individual experiences the unpleasant consequences even once. In such situations the punishment might be of little effect in preventing the behavior which produced it. Repeating our cigarette example, smoking may very well lead to painful illness and early death. These consequences are delayed effects, and when they do occur, it is too late. It is, in a sense, impossible to learn to avoid cigarettes.

Thus, from the simple observation that time delay interferes with learning, we may conclude that an immediate pleasant outcome can override even a large but delayed unpleasant one and the trap will be entered. Moreover, this can be so even if in some quantitative sense the unpleasant consequences are disastrous (as they are in the case of smoking) while the attractions are only relatively moderate (as, indeed, many smokers feel they are). In the particular case of cigarettes, both the public pronouncements as to the dangers of smoking and the occasional observation of someone else suffering its agonizing consequences are anxiety-producing events. They may produce some avoidance, but neither has a tangible physical impact to compete with the pleasant consequences, nor do they occur frequently in close temporal proximity to the act of smoking itself. Except in the case of persons who are strongly susceptible to suggestion or who are very conscientious about their future health, the consequences are not adequate to keep one out of the trap.

Time-delay countertraps are equally common. An example is found in the case of the high school dropout who, avoiding the present pain and unpleasantness of school, finds himself later lacking the education which could have prepared him for a more rewarding job. Despite a widespread recognition of this problem, the proposals for dealing with it are not very constructive. Most attempts to discourage dropping out are confined to propaganda efforts designed to convince students of the potential value of a high school diploma, promising those who stay substantial economic gains at some vague time in the future. As in the case of public warnings against cigarettes, we would expect such pronouncements to have only a marginal effect. Instead of counteracting the bait in the trap by reducing those aversive elements of school that drive some students into the trapped behavior, the statements serve only to describe the punishment associated with the trap itself. Since this is, at best, an addition to the undesirable consequence of dropping out which itself occurs some time in the future, there is no reason to expect the strategy to meet with much success. Such statements serve only to increase the threat of a future loss, and to the extent that they have any tangible reinforcing power, will only frustrate the individual who is now faced with aversive stimuli whichever way he turns. In social-trap terms, the dropout is not an ignorant person who fails to plan his future, but simply someone confronted by immediate and present reinforcers that point the wrong way—to a mode of behavior which will be regretted later on.

The attenuation of learning due to time delays is recognized by most social scientists today. Among many psychologists, it is seen as a fundamental property of the learning process (which in turn is critical in the determination of all human behavior). Among economists, too, the importance of time factors is commonly taken into account, and the observed fact that delayed payoffs have a markedly reduced influence over

behavior has been built into all major economic theories dealing with decision making over time. This being the case, it is
surprising that the role of time delay in the acquisition of
unreasonable or even dangerous patterns of behavior has not
been given more emphasis by these specialists. Economists,
particularly, have skirted the issue through the development
of models which have an extremely rationalistic character, incorporating the notions that individuals consciously plan their
actions and take full account of all the known future consequences of their behavior. The observed deemphasis of future
events in the determination of any course of action is then
seen to be the result of deliberate decision making, rather than
the consequence of an inherently myopic choice mechanism.
What we view as a potentially serious trap is not seen by the
economist to be any problem at all, but merely an interesting
aspect of the decision-making process. Our objections to this
viewpoint will be made more explicit in the following chapter.

Ignorance Traps

According to the legend, King Midas turned many objects into
gold before discovering that his dinner would suffer the same
transformation. The king was neatly trapped: the attractiveness of the offered power to convert ordinary objects into
riches drew him into an agreement with disastrous consequences that should have been obvious. The interesting feature of the story and the moral it is intended to stress is that
the king's greed (the extraordinary attractiveness of the bait)
actually *precluded* a rational evaluation of the situation. Generally, it seems to be fairly common that highly attractive reinforcers have the effect of inhibiting even ordinary reflections
upon the consequences of one's behavior. Thus the beautiful
new car or the wonderful new house may be well beyond the
purchaser's means, but in the excitement of the moment it is
hard to calculate mortgage payments, maintenance costs, and
fuel bills.

We name this class of traps ignorance traps since they represent a failure to accept or utilize generally available knowledge when making a choice between alternative actions. In contrast to a time-delay trap, in which the existence of a future punishment may be readily acknowledged ("Boy, am I going to be hung over tomorrow!" or "Lend me a 'cancer stick' "), an ignorance trap could be easily avoided were the existence of the punishment properly comprehended by the victim. The ignorance countertrap occurs when the positive consequence of a rational action is not recognized and an aversion to the negative consequence leads the individual to select an inferior behavior instead. "Try it, you'll like it" is the catch phrase of those who believe their friends to be caught in such traps, and if the "it" is innocuous, such as trying calves brains in a restaurant, they may be right.

As we use it, the ignorance-trap category incorporates a number of different learning phenomena. It includes the Midas case in which the magnitude of the positive reinforcer seems to preclude even the most elementary analysis of the situation. Also included are superstition traps in which a reward happens to occur coincidentally with an action, when in fact they are unrelated. The chance event reinforces the action, though common sense would belie the connection. A third subclass is the intermittent reinforcer trap. It is a property of reinforcement learning that behavior that is conditioned by intermittent rewards is much more persistent than behavior brought about by regularly occurring reinforcers. Thus the victim may be induced to repeat behavior which, in the long run, is inferior to its alternatives. This third case is often cited as an explanation for compulsive gambling behavior: the occasional wins that occur in a series of repeated gambles reinforce the behavior to a degree far out of proportion to the amount of reward received by the gambler.

Going beyond these elementary cases, ignorance traps are unified by the extraordinary human capacity for developing and acting upon theories which describe supposed natural properties of the world. If it is the implementation of a theory that is learned through the mechanisms of reinforcement rather than simply a few elements of behavior, the ignorance trap may be extended into a broad variety of new and unfamiliar situations. As in the case of most of our different classes of traps, the properties of reinforcement learning that make ignorance traps possible are already recognized by psychologists. In particular, the extraordinary power of intermittent rewards to influence behavior has been extensively evaluated and commented upon. The other elements of the ignorance-trap theory (such as the Midas effect, superstition, and particularly the capacity of abstract reasoning for generalizing patterns of behavior) have been less thoroughly investigated, although references to them are nevertheless not difficult to find. There is certainly nothing new to the observation that ignorance—even of this peculiarly self-imposed kind—is at the root of many of our problems. Indeed, it is such a ready explanation for all kinds of inappropriate or ineffective behavior that it is undoubtedly overused as an explanation for a variety of social ills. Certainly it would be an oversimplification to assert that international conflict, high school dropouts, cigarette smoking, and drug addiction were all basically the result of ignorance. We prefer to confine this term to the narrowly specified circumstances already described.

Sliding-Reinforcer Traps

According to theatrical portrayals, Henry VIII courted Katherine Howard with the same vigor that had characterized the courtships of his youth. He rode, danced, drank, and generally carried on after the fashion of a spirited twenty-year-old. Once married, however, he was forced to acknowledge to himself and his bride that he was actually a sick old man.

Learning is a time-consuming process, and any specific kind of behavior may require several reinforcements before becoming established as a habit. Once established, however, a habit may persist without further positive reinforcements or even in the presence of punishments. Some patterns of behavior continue long after the circumstances under which that behavior was appropriate have ceased to be relevant, producing negative consequences that would have been avoided easily had the behavior stopped earlier. In the sliding-reinforcer trap, any given instance of an action does not necessarily produce multiple consequences. There may, instead, be a period of time or a sequence of events during which the behavior is accompanied by rewards only, followed by a period of time or sequence of events during which the behavior is followed by only punishments. The trap occurs because the rewards establish a habit which persists in the succeeding period. In essence, these are traps that have been baited by success.

Sometimes the shift of the outcome from reward to punishment is a consequence of the behavior itself. A child who sings "Row, Row, Row Your Boat" for the first time will be greeted with parental praise and encouragement, and so naturally the song is sung again and is encouraged again. With repetitions, however, the adult enthusiasm will have diminished markedly; indeed, the fifteenth rendition is likely to inspire active punishment. Other than the fact that it is the behavior itself which alters the reinforcement structure, however, this example is little different from our first case.

A more complicated (and more dangerous) form of the trap arises when the behavior not only alters its own consequences, but alters the consequences of alternative behaviors as well. In the simple example of the child's song, it is always possible to escape from the punishment by breaking the habit and choosing another behavior, such as not singing. But if it should happen that the consequences of such an alternative are transformed into punishment by the repetition of the trapped behavior itself, then the option of escape through the alternative may be lost. Such may be the case, for example, for an individual who is given the opportunity to consume a potentially addictive drug. Abstention may actually be less "rational" than one-time consumption; that is, a single dose has few detrimental effects and may have a positively reinforcing physiological impact. Thus one-time use is more strongly rewarded than is abstention, the consequences of which are neutral. Drug use tends to alter these values, however, and after successive occasions, abstention becomes painful, even though the pleasures of consumption are also reduced. Thus, although the rewards are eliminated and replaced by the debilitating effects of drug use, the behavior still dominates because of the new aversive stimulus associated with stopping. The individual is left in a far worse condition than he would have been if abstention had been the behavior all along; yet, at each step along the way, indulgence was chosen—either because it was positively reinforced or because abstention produced punishments sufficient to drive the individual back to the drug. Simple termination of a behavioral habit is by no means sufficient to escape from this form of the trap.

Sliding-reinforcer countertraps can arise in similar forms. In one form, aversion to an undesirable outcome leads to selection of some behavior, and the repeated success of that behavior in avoiding the unpleasantness reinforces it until it becomes habitual. The trap arises if repetition of the behavior that originally led to punishment is capable of producing great rewards over time. The trap might appear in the form of a simple phobia: a few unpleasant experiences in a childhood swimming pool might lead to a persistent avoidance of the seashore forever after. A more complicated form occurs if it is the repetition itself which modifies the reinforcements. A child who must practice in order to learn to play a musical instrument is confronted at first with an unpleasant experience accompanied by few rewards. As the child becomes proficient, however, the rewards increase while the practice becomes less unpleasant. If the initial aversion prevents practice, the child is in a trap. In such cases, the trapped behavior itself diminishes the payoffs and exacerbates the trap. The child who has acquired limited proficiency on his instrument may still find that the pains of practice exceed the pleasures of performance. If, in discouragement, he abandons the instrument for awhile, his competence will deteriorate and the rewards of playing will be further reduced, thereby restoring the original unpleasantness of practice. Thus, avoidance of practice increases the pressures to further avoidance. This, of course, is the countertrap version of the drug-addiction example.

To the best of our knowledge, the sliding-reinforcer trap is one type not systematically studied heretofore within the social sciences. These are situations in which the circumstances under which future decisions are made are themselves determined by current behavior. Even in economics, where the mathematical properties of such decision problems are recognized, only the simplest kinds of models have been investigated analytically. The problems of drug and alcohol dependence are themselves subjects of an enormous literature, but an association with our more general class of problems is not made. The increasing public interest in the preservation of our environment focuses attention upon another area of application: the growing immunity of insect pests to various insecticides, the gradual destruction of our natural environment, and the wasteful overuse of energy resources are all situations in which the habits established by repeated successes in the past have begun to outlive their usefulness and may become seriously damaging instead.

Externality Traps

Time-delay traps, ignorance traps, and sliding-reinforcer traps have all been characterized with reference to the consequences of a victim's own actions. These are all individual traps in that the punishments faced by any one person need not depend upon the behavior of other potential victims. They become social traps when many victims are caught in parallel (such as cases of excessive smoking and alcoholism), when escapes from individual traps are influenced by social action (such as our willingness to permit or prohibit cigarette advertising or to outlaw drug use), or when there is a great deal of interaction among victims of the same trap. Cigarette smokers often encourage one another in the habit (indeed, smoking often commences under conditions of peer group pressure), and the sight of many others smoking may have the effect of calming one's own anxiety about its consequences—after all, all of those people must know what they are doing. Gamblers, similarly, may be excited by the sight of another's winnings (the coins spilling out of the slot machine) and thus be reinforced in their own trapped behavior.

There exist other forms of trap in which social interaction provides the fundamental mechanisms so that in the absence of a multiperson society they could not occur at all. Since the nineteenth century, economists have debated the merits of situations in which one individual, acting in his own interest, makes decisions that have an incidental impact upon the welfare of others. Contemporary economists have contrived the term "externality" to describe this condition, reflecting the fact that one person's behavior may have consequences "external" to his own sphere of interest. Rather than devise a new term for such an old problem, we have used it for the title of our fourth trap. If one person's behavior directly influences the welfare of another, a trap can arise because the reinforcements that are relevant to the first individual may not coincide with the returns received by the second. If Peter spends five minutes in a cafeteria line choosing his dessert, he does not suffer for it, but all the people waiting behind him certainly do. The structure of the situation has made it possible for him to make a decision that is binding on others: if he chooses to go slowly through the line, so must those behind him.

This trap designation is not intended to refer to circumstances in which a person has been elected to a decision-making position; it applies to situations in which he has influence merely because of some technical or happenstance element in the structure of the situation itself. Peter was not elected to his position in the cafeteria line, and since he has simply taken his turn, there is little which those waiting behind him can do, no matter how unsatisfactory his behavior may be from their point of view.

Externality countertraps are defined as those cases in which one person's avoidance of an action leaves others worse off than they would have been had that action been undertaken, or, alternatively, when one individual has the power to improve the welfare of others but the reinforcers that confront him discourage the necessary action. To some suburban homeowners, the labor and expense of outside maintenance reinforce the avoidance of upkeep and repair. While this state may be satisfactory to the householder, it certainly is not satisfactory to the neighbors, who then must put up with a local eyesore.

Externality traps are often said to be attributable only to a narrowly defined concept of "economic man" and to arise only in the case of highly self-interested individuals who have no sympathy for the needs of others. By shifting the focus to the learning process—in which the emphasis is not upon motive, but upon perceived behavioral successes—we hope to show that the problem is much more general than such a view would imply. The learning process does admit the possibility that improvements in the welfare of others can be reinforcing for oneself, and some externality traps can be alleviated to the extent that this is the case. Indeed, techniques for enhancing the connection between the consequences to self and others hold great potential as a remedy for these traps. Altruism alone, however, is an imperfect source of escape from these traps. The extent to which it is reinforcing is unlikely to be commensurate with the magnitude of the externality: if it is too small, the trap is only diminished and not eliminated; if it is too large, a new trap is created in which one individual suffers punishments for the sake of insignificant benefits to others. Indeed, as any child of extremely indulgent parents can testify, an overoptimistic view of the good that one's behavior does for others is as capable of leading into traps as is an utter indifference.

Collective Traps

The influence of an externality trap can be expanded substantially when there are several individuals behaving symmetrically, each in a position to influence the welfare of the others.

With more participants, the losses attributable to externality traps can be very large, even if the simple externality component—the magnitude of the harm that one person's action may impose upon someone else—is quite trivial.

Suppose Peter is an enthusiastic outdoor chef and has established a rather smoky barbecue in his backyard. When he broils a steak, he suffers a little from the smoke, but he benefits a great deal from the steak. His neighbors also suffer from the smoke, but they get none of his steak. This is an externality problem to the extent that Peter's behavior is conditioned by reinforcements that do not reflect the slight punishments imposed upon others, although the smoke may not be so serious that his neighbors actually resent his hobby. Suppose, however, that everyone on Peter's block follows his example and decides to barbecue outdoors. The resulting aggregation of smoke from twenty to thirty outdoor barbecues may now impose serious discomfort upon everyone. Indeed, even the originally enthusiastic Peter may now maintain that the smoke is such a nuisance that he and everyone else should seal off their outdoor cookers and prepare their meals inside, using more conventional apparatus. Even so, each individual cook-out produces only a fractional increase in the overall level of pollution, and thus each amateur chef still finds that the pleasure of his own activity outweighs its contribution to his personal feelings of discomfort. The neighborhood is in a trap, not because any one individual is acting against the public interest, but because the public, as a collectivity, is acting against the public interest.

Many cases of environmental pollution provide examples of this sort of trap: it may be convenient and easy to dispose of waste in the nearest river, and one individual doing so does not noticeably degrade the river for other uses; but when everybody uses a river in this way, its usefulness is dramatically reduced. Indeed, the trap may be compounded in that the reinforcements contingent upon one's own behavior are themselves dependent upon the actions of others. That is, one may experience a tinge of regret when dumping waste into a clean river, and hence that behavior might be inhibited; but, once the river is polluted, even that "punishment" disappears and the situation is worsened.

Just as the collective trap is an extension of the simple externality trap, so the collective countertrap is an extension of the externality countertrap. One individual may avoid behavior that is costly to himself but which does slight amounts of good to others without being said to have created much of a trap, because the external benefits may be trivial. But a trivial countertrap may become significant if many individuals taking the same action would generate benefits worth the personal cost required to achieve them.

An example can again be taken from Peter and his neighbors. If Peter is the only resident on a northern New England city street who shovels snow from his sidewalk in winter, then he suffers the discomfort of hard work yet gains little benefit from having a place to walk because the rest of the sidewalk is still covered. The neighbors also benefit slightly from Peter's cleared section, but with most of the sidewalk still impassable, that benefit is insignificant. Under the circumstances it would be understandable if Peter stopped shoveling. The same is true for each of his neighbors, so the sidewalk may never be cleared. Yet every householder on the street may feel that if he could be assured of an entirely cleared walk, he would willingly make his own contribution; if everyone were to clear his own section, then the benefit would be magnified into something substantial for all. Like the barbecue example, this countertrap is not so much a case of individuals failing to act in the public interest as it is of the public failing to act in the public interest.

It is indicative of the importance of collective externality traps that, in addition to the extensive economics literature that exists on the subject, the problem has been rediscovered in at least two other branches of the social sciences. Early in the development of the theory of games, a paradigm known as the "prisoner's dilemma" (a simple two-person analog to our outdoor barbecue example) was developed and has since served as the focus of a great deal of interesting and important empirical experimentation. More recently still, Garrett Hardin has popularized an elementary form of the same phenomenon under the rubric of the "tragedy of the commons." It is a sad testimony to the lack of communication among members of different professions that the growing and sophisticated economics literature which exists on this subject should be so completely overlooked by others and, conversely, that the experimental data now available have not had any tangible impact upon the formulation of the economic theory.

Hybrid Traps

Some traps are mixtures of our five classifications, and in many cases it is possible to identify all of the elements combined into one problem area. For example, consider just a few of the problems surrounding international armament, confrontation, and conflict. There is certainly a time-delay mechanism at work: early in a conflict, a nation may be willing to escalate its involvement simply because it fails to give sufficient weight to the enormous costs the conflict will ultimately impose. Compounding this may be an ignorance component, insofar as objective studies of the possible consequences of a conflict are actually avoided. The sliding-reinforcer trap enters when an armament buildup reflects a response that may have been previously appropriate but is no longer so. (An example is the enormous expansion of nuclear capabilities by the major powers during the fifties and sixties, when in fact the conflicts that arose took the form of conventional and guerilla warfare.) The externality trap arises since many people who influence the course of international events are not subject to the same reinforcers as are other members of the population. (It is often observed, for example, that within the military, experience in battle is a valuable asset for eventual promotion; to career military men, widespread and continuing peace is not the blessing it may appear to be to others.) Finally, the arms race also embodies a multi-person trap. Each nation may well consider itself to be threatened not by only one potential enemy, but by an aggregation of potential enemies. Thus it must defend itself not just against the arms buildup of one potential foe, but against the arms of all potential foes.

We might include in the class of hybrid traps those initially simple traps that have been compounded by misguided legislative or administrative attempts at escape. Often such attempts succeed only in superimposing a new trap on top of the old one. For example, until about a hundred years ago common debtors were imprisoned, adding physical entrapment to their other problems and making repayment of debts less likely. Today we sometimes do the same to those caught in drug traps, adding the punishment of imprisonment to the ones they already suffer. Or, when we attempt to control gambling through legal sanctions, we may succeed only in driving the operations underground, providing more lucrative rewards to those willing to violate the law. We trap ourselves by creating a situation in which important sources of revenue flow to the least responsible members of our own society. Such examples are numerous, suggesting that one of the important objectives of an analysis of traps must be the development of cures which are not worse than the diseases.

Despite the complexity of hybrid traps, we have not encountered any cases that differ in their fundamentals from a simple summation of the basic traps they contain, which encourages us in the belief that traps are not qualitatively changed when they are combined with one another and that our five basic types are adequate for describing trapped behavior in general. The main problems to be confronted in hybrid cases are their complexity and the possibility of exacerbating the trap through imperfect escapes, rather than any new feature of traps themselves.

Alternative Taxonomies

We are well aware that there are other possible ways of structuring our taxonomy. We could distinguish traps involving only individuals from those which arise from interdependence among individuals; traps in which the problem is social from traps in which only the solution is social; or static traps, in which all reinforcers occur more or less simultaneously, from dynamic traps, in which the passage of time plays an essential part. These distinctions are made in our discussions when they become relevant. We have chosen the preceding form of taxonomy largely because it seemed simpler and more convenient to distinguish traps according to their causes rather than according to what seem to be essentially descriptive details. Our taxonomy also results in fewer categories, making it much easier to assign perceived social problems to proper trap classes.

In spite of these considerations, we have not entirely succeeded in following a single principle for our taxonomy. For example, although ignorance traps comprise not one but three different causes, it is more convenient to classify together those static traps that manifestly conflict with scientific rationality than to divide them into three minor types. Similarly, externality traps and collective traps both stem from the same ultimate cause: the potential of one individual's behavior for affecting the welfare of another. In this case it was the great qualitative differences between simple externality traps and those which arise only from collective behavior that motivated the distinction. Such deviations from principle are intended only as concessions to utility and are not to be viewed as compromises with alternative possible taxonomies.

Ways Out

Discussion of the escapes and remedies that can be applied to social traps must be deferred until the traps themselves have been more fully described, but we can provide at this point a summary outline of the direction our arguments will take. Consistent with the view that inappropriate reinforcement structures give rise to traps, our basic procedure will be to look for ways to modify existing reinforcers or to supplement them with new ones, thereby directing behavior away from the trap and into more successful channels. The traps we have outlined are not new discoveries, but instead reflect a new perspective on social problems. Consequently, the escapes will be found, in most cases, to be quite familiar. Our objective will be to show how a variety of practical mechanisms for dealing with these problems fits into our general framework and how the potential merits of each can be evaluated from the point of view of learning theory. Although we will suggest a few new escapes and some modifications of old ones, the effectiveness of such innovations must remain largely speculative, the alternatives having been derived mostly from learning theory rather than from substantial experimental data. Reliable empirical evidence is quite limited once we turn to procedures for changing a situation in which a trap may arise. Although we are confident that the principles of learning we apply are appropriate, nevertheless our list of remedies relies more heavily on the logic of the situations than does our list of traps themselves.

Certainly the most promising approach to any trap problem would be to present reinforcers in a manner that would direct behavior along rational paths by eliminating the biases introduced by time delay, ignorance, or even the fact that the consequences of one's behavior may fall on someone else. This procedure would convert a trap into a trade-off, presenting the individual with a set of reinforcers that occur in close proximity to the behavior in question and which closely match the actual reward and punishment patterns that underly the situation. The trap then becomes a simple choice situation in which rational and learned behavior are coincident. In some cases—particularly those of time-delay traps—this might be accomplished simply by altering the timing of reinforcers, somehow bringing the punishment or a proxy for the punishment into closer proximity with its causative behavior. In many cases, however, one would have to supplement old reinforcers with new ones, using social, economic, or political influences to counter the behavioral bias introduced by the bait.

A less satisfactory approach to the problems created by traps is to give victims some shelter from the punishments. Just as automobile insurance compensates accident victims for their loss, so one can compensate the victims of traps. To the extent that single mothers are the victims of traps, the various social child-support programs now in existence represent at least partial moves in this direction. However, shelters are by no means completely effective remedies; they can ameliorate traps, but since they do nothing to counter the bait that is responsible for the trap in the first place, the underlying problem is not resolved.

In the extreme, traps may be avoided simply by depriving people of the power to enter them. Had Prohibition succeeded in cutting off the supply of alcohol to consumers, the whole range of traps from the simple drink hangover to outright alcoholism would have been forestalled. Similarly, were we able to cut off the importation of opiates and the distribution of manufactured drugs within the United States, drug traps would no longer pose the threat they do now. Nevertheless, legal barriers to traps do not usually seem to work. In the first place, their inflexibility leads them to constrain the behavior of untrapped and trapped alike, depriving nonvictims of socially harmless rewards. Prohibition, by attempting to prevent everyone from drinking, imposed a social cost of its own; and because it applied to so many people, the cost of the cure may have even exceeded the social cost of the trap it was intended to remedy. Second, use of rigid legislative devices often does nothing more than compound simple traps, causing potentially more serious hybrid traps. Thus, both Prohibition and the banning of drug importation appear to have been relatively ineffective in dealing with their respective social traps. Contrarily, by transforming the clandestine manufacture and distribution of these commodities into highly profitable ventures, such laws have provided unethical segments of the society with a valuable economic base. In effect, such policies supplement bad traps with worse ones.

A reinterpretation of social problems as multiple-reinforcer traps also alters the role one might give to the educational process as a means of solution. It is apparent that merely to instruct someone that a trap exists or that he is in one is not, in itself, sufficient to bring about a resolution of the problem. The basic reinforcements are still operating, and in most cases a purely intellectual understanding of their nature will accomplish very little in the way of weakening their capacity to shape behavior. Indeed, some modes of education may actually be counterproductive in that they weaken an aversive stimulus that was formerly of assistance in avoiding the trap. For example, many teenagers may avoid experimentation with drugs because they have been led to believe that drug use has immediate and disastrous consequences. The belief may be entirely false, but however artificial this reinforcer may be, it does contribute to avoidance of the trap. A drug education course correcting the misapprehension may serve only to relieve the fear and reassure the student that "experimentation" will not have immediate or serious consequences. The threat of the long-term consequences of addiction is ineffective because it is clear that addiction is not an inevitable consequence of one- or two-time indulgence, and besides, the punishment is long delayed. Thus, by removing a negative reinforcer, drug education may actually lead to increased drug use.

Many psychologists believe that the only efficient way to unlearn a habit is to learn (be rewarded for) behavior that interferes with that habit. According to this view, once a habit has been acquired it will persist indefinitely, even if the reinforcement stops. Only if a punishment is imposed or (what is formally similar) some alternative activity is rewarded will the behavior cease. This suggests that education could combat social traps by providing reinforcements for those particular forms of behavior that interfere with entry into traps.

It may be obvious that certain events (such as a hungry child's receiving food, or finding shelter during a rainstorm) are inherently rewarding, but many of our daily rewards are, in fact, socially and culturally acquired. Many rewards require preliminary preparation to be effective. Listening to a symphony and looking at a Picasso are most strongly reinforcing after one has expanded one's understanding of music and art. A traditional function of education has been the development of social and cultural capacities for enjoyment, and before the twentieth century, at least, this was apparently accepted as a primary function of education. Moreover, the behaviors reinforced by these cultural rewards often prove to conflict with those that lead into traps. For example, a drug- or alcohol-induced state of intoxication is incompatible with effective social intercourse, and if we regard intelligent, sophisticated conversation as pleasant, then inebriation is no longer a state to be desired. We have already noted that if the welfare of others is made to be reinforcing, externality traps will tend to be reduced in intensity. Here, too, the educational system provides an appropriate mechanism for heightening interpersonal sensitivity. The obvious implication is that a simple and satisfactory way to escape traps is to stimulate behavior that forestalls entry into them in the first place.

Finally, we hope it is clear why we believe that analyses of social dilemmas relying upon the identification of ignorant or guilty parties are grossly oversimplified. Indeed, this attitude often leads to proposed remedies that simply compound the trap. People are caught in traps not because they are stupid or their motives are bad, but because the reinforcers they face are providing improper guides for behavior. Our responsibility here is to improve the route signs, rather than to castigate the driver for getting lost.

3

Time-Delay Traps

Death and the Young Man

Housebook Master
drypoint c. 1480

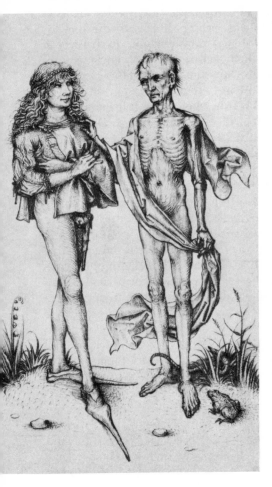

This image of an elegant young man confronted by death serves as a dramatic fifteenth-century reminder that it is a mistake to ignore the future.

A dentist offers a child a lollipop as a reward for good behavior in his office; this serves the purpose of maintaining good working conditions for him and, incidentally, increases the future demand for his services. But suppose instead of an immediate lollipop, he promises to mail one along with his bill on the first day of the next month. Surely such a tardy reward would be less effective in eliciting cooperative behavior from the child in the dentist's chair.

The intuitive impression that a postponement in delivery of the lollipop would virtually eliminate its effectiveness as a reward is well supported by experimental studies of learning, and it is generally accepted that time delays will greatly lessen the reinforcing power of rewards, even when it is known with certainty that the rewards will eventually occur. Delaying a punishment also reduces the impact: the certainty of tomorrow's hangover does not always inhibit today's drinking.

The attenuation of effect of rewards and punishments with time delay has a fundamental place in the economic theory of interest-rate determination. The willingness to borrow money for consumption, often at substantial rates of interest, implies a willingness to incur debts which, in total, exceed the value of the money received in the present; and this is only possible if future obligations are not weighted as heavily in one's concerns as are current purchases. Of course, borrowing for investment is quite rational because the investment yields a return of its own which may be more than sufficient to cover the debt. Nevertheless, one often encounters individuals who go far beyond rational investment, borrowing so much for the sake of current consumption that they subject themselves to catastrophic future debts. In 1932, the great American economist Irving Fisher associated this behavior with "impatience," a personality trait he defined as reflecting an undervaluation of the future compared to the present. Fisher himself was inclined to attribute this impatience to a lack of foresight and self-control. From his point of view, the man who fails to save any money during his years of employment and finds himself at the point of starvation at retirement is simply very foolish.

He put it quite bluntly: "A weak will usually goes with a weak intellect."

Such harsh judgment upon the plight of those who do not prepare for their futures is by no means unique to economists. The same general attitude is conventionally expressed toward school dropouts, single mothers, heavy installment buyers, lazy students, overweight gluttons, and cigarette smokers. Our folklore reflects the same point of view: the hardworking ant survives the winter because he prepared for it, while the happy-go-lucky grasshopper must finally face the consequences of his indolence. According to this attitude, those who suffer the consequences of shortsightedness are merely paying for their own behavior: the punishments they face are of their own choosing and are not imposed by any outside agency. Ironically, this unsympathetic popular view is itself based upon the optimistic premise that human behavior is (or should be) determined by a goal-oriented intellectual process of evaluating alternative destinations and then following the path to the best one, rather than on the simpler and more direct procedure of permitting immediate rewards and punishments to dictate direction. If we encounter someone who is suffering from a failure to save for the future, we are too often led to criticize that person's intelligence and willpower, instead of understanding him to be the victim of a trap. The inadequate connection of future consequences with present behavior is fundamentally responsible for insufficient preparation for the future, and while Fisher may have been correct in maintaining that persons with great self-control and intelligence are likely to be effective planners, possession of these qualities is only one of several means available for avoiding the trap.

Occasionally one encounters an extreme, rationalistic view of the effects of time delay. Among contemporary economists, particularly, a view has become prevalent to the effect that the general tendency to downgrade the importance of the future is not due to a lack of foresight or planning, but rather is the consequence of deliberate policy, reflecting the characteristics of preferences themselves. According to this theory, the future is intentionally given less weight than the present because it actually is less important from the individual's point of view; hence, even a fully informed, intelligent decision maker, with all requisite self-control, may demonstrate a marked preference for present goods over future goods. A practical consequence of this interpretation has been that empirical evidence of behavior which downgrades the future (willingness to smoke in the face of its health hazards, for example) is not regarded as a social problem, but instead is viewed as a property of rational choice. From this point of view, the man who has failed to prepare for retirement is seen to be suffering, but only because he so chose, having deliberately decided earlier that the suffering was a fair price to pay for what might have appeared to an outsider to be excessive spending during his working lifetime. The importance of this super-rationalistic view is that it denies the very existence of time-delay traps. After all, it is characteristic of all of our traps that they incorporate both rewards and punishments, and in the absence of any empirical index of the relative magnitudes of these payoffs, it is often possible to put forward an argument to the effect that the preferred choice is the one being made, hence that no trap is involved.

The most direct means for refuting this challenge—the precise quantification of the relevant rewards—is, in most cases, not yet available to modern science. Nevertheless there does exist evidence which can be used to challenge the rationalist view. In practice, economists distinguish the present from the future by intervals largely measured in terms of years, and it is implicit in their models that very short time delays (such as those measured in minutes or days) should have but slight effects upon choice behavior. This theoretical view is in direct conflict with experimental evidence from psychological studies which indicate that even short delays will significantly inhibit learning. It is found, for example, that reversal in the temporal order of a sequence of reinforcers that occur in fairly close proximity will alter learned behavior dramatically. These experiments, unfortunately, are subject to the criticism that they rely too heavily upon animal experiments to be conclusive indicators of human behavior; nevertheless, a human analog to a reversal in a sequence of rewards may be imagined.

Peter occasionally goes to a party, drinks heavily, and then suffers a painful hangover the following morning. Suppose the order of the sequence could be reversed, so that Peter first chose a hangover that would be followed later by the pleasure of the drinks. The hangover might be brought on by consumption of special pills: in the morning, Peter could take, say, five of these pills and suffer immediately whatever ill effects he normally suffers from five drinks. He can then enjoy five cocktails, or their alcoholic equivalent, at any time during the day or evening, followed by no symptoms of hangover whatever. The sixth drink during that day will have precisely the same taste and physiological effect as ordinary icewater unless a sixth pill has been taken earlier, accompanied of course by appropriately heightened symptoms of hangover. If it is true that a drink-hangover sequence is not a trap, as the rationalists would have it, this reversal in sequence between drinks and hangovers would have no effect whatever on the overall level of drinking (except, of course, in the event of unanticipated occasions for socializing, for which one might be permitted access to old-fashioned alcohol). The time lag between drink and hangover, whichever comes first, is much too short for the rational "discounting" process to have any significant impact. One's intuition, like the psychological learning experiments, however, provides no support for such a prediction. Peter might decide, the morning before a social event, that certainly two drinks will be sufficient for the day and thus take only two of the pills. In the evening, however, one can expect to hear expressions of regret that the opportunity for conviviality could not be adequately exploited because of an insufficient consumption of the necessary pills.

Further evidence that time-delay traps operate routinely in drinking situations is provided by the wide variations in attitude as a victim progresses through a trap. During a party, the forthcoming hangover is small on the horizon and the rewards

of drink are praised in deed, if not in word. During the hangover, the pleasure of the drink is forgotten and, in an extreme
case, alcohol may even be sworn off forever. In neither of
these periods is there much incentive for evaluation of the
experience as a whole; consequently, resolutions made during
them (to go to more parties or never to drink again) are likely
to be forgotten very soon. Only during intervening periods,
free of both parties and hangovers, is one capable of making a
reasonable evaluation of the consequences of one's own behavior. Resolutions made during the hangover never to drink
again are, of course, later recognized as shortsighted in the
same sense that the excessive drinking was shortsighted.

In general, when confronted by cyclic situations such as this
(a pleasurable state followed by a painful state followed by a
period of reflection before the cycle begins again), we learn to
develop personal rules of thumb and to appreciate social
norms that constrain our behavior to patterns consistent with
our overall welfare. Thus we may establish conventions for
ourselves that prevent the bait in potential traps from drawing
us in too far: "Two is my limit" or "Never mix your drinks"
are typical examples for dealing with alcohol. In spite of these
rules, we believe that such traps are still not completely
avoided; even in cyclic situations, many people continue to
obey short-term reinforcers more than, in reflective moments,
they would like to. This point of view is encouraged by the
intuitive appeal of the hangover reversal example. Even if the
hangover came first, most people would learn not to permit
that short-run punishment to deprive them of all of the pleasure of drinking, but it is surely unlikely that they would
prepare themselves for as much drinking as occurs under present-day circumstances, when the hangover is second in the
sequence. Just as people sometimes overindulge now, we
would encounter underindulgence. The mechanism of revers-
ing the order of the reinforcers would transform a simple time-
delay trap into a simple time-delay countertrap, and neither of
these can be entirely avoided.

If such simple traps sometimes catch us, in spite of rules of thumb and social norms which help to avoid them, then they will be all the more potent where conventional constraints have not been developed. The experience of the American Indians with alcohol provides an interesting case in point. At the time of the arrival of the early settlers, the Indians had had no exposure to distilled alcohol and consequently had developed no social rules for avoiding its associated traps. When presented by the settlers with "firewater," they frequently drank themselves into stupors that in some cases led to death. Indeed, the Indians' inability to control their alcohol consumption was so apparent that dispensing liquor to them was made a crime in many communities. Moreover, that they were caught in a trap is the only reasonable explanation for the Indians' behavior, it being specious to maintain that they were unaware of the consequences of excessive drinking (the first good hangover is sufficient for that); and it is absurd to take the rationalist view, maintaining that they chose to drink heavily, openly accepting its eventual consequences.

The more recent experience of United States soldiers in Vietnam provides a similar example. Opiates have routinely been available in Southeast Asia for many years, long enough to permit the Vietnamese society to develop rules and conventions for avoiding drug traps. Our GIs, however, lacked experience; consequently, drug abuse was common in the United States Army, but not in the armies of either North or South Vietnam.

Doomsday Traps

Most of our examples have described recurrent traps, in which the sequence of behavior-reward-punishment repeats itself often enough to permit the accumulation of some experience with the problem as a whole. The importance of this recurrence is that it permits the evolution of constraining conventions that encourage avoidance. "Two drinks is my limit" and "Never drink on an empty stomach" are useful guides to behavior, as well as reflections of personal experience. The less experience one has with a trap, the less able one is to develop such rules. Moreover, experience may be required before the existence of the trap is even recognized and the necessity for such rules appreciated. Thus, the less frequent the recurrence of a trap or the longer the time lag between the behavior and its punishment, the more difficult it will be to develop avoidance conventions. From the point of view of the individual, the cigarette-smoking trap is a difficult one to escape because the punishment for smoking occurs so long after smoking begins that the individual has no opportunity to learn techniques of avoidance. Indeed, once having encountered the punishment, the smoker may have no incentive for giving up the habit—the damage has already been done. Individual experience gives little opportunity to learn how to deal with the smoking trap; instead, avoidance depends upon one generation passing its experience on to another, or the scientific community somehow succeeding in convincing people of the seriousness or inevitability of the consequences of smoking.

We may describe as a doomsday trap the extreme case in which the time lag is so long or the punishment so catastrophic that avoidance learning is impossible. Such a trap may not be recognized until the victim is already hopelessly subjected to a punishment produced by actions long since completed and now irreversible. The smoker, the prodigal son who squanders his patrimony, the high school dropout, and the young offender who colors his entire future through imprisonment in a penal institution are all victims of traps with a common element of fatal permanency. Since individual learning is difficult without repeated experience, avoidance of doomsday traps is as much a social as an individual problem. Only within the experience of an entire society are these traps recursive: there are many smokers, many prodigals, many school dropouts, and many young offenders, and their experiences are repeated in many successive generations. Thus, learning that is beyond the individual's experience is available to society as a whole. Many of us may be in a position to observe and "learn" from the experiences of others who are already victims, and this can facilitate the recognition of traps and generate some incentive to search for means of avoidance, but the experience yielded by such observations is very limited and may even be colored by happenstance features that are misleading as to the nature of a trap and its seriousness. On the whole, we see collective action as the only effective means for avoiding doomsday traps.

Although social action may be required, it is nevertheless possible that it is the society itself which is trapped. One increasingly hears predictions of social catastrophe following an anticipated exhaustion of our mineral and energy resources. Once those resources are gone, it is argued, it will be too late to do anything about it. Some examples of this kind of problem are already well known: we may disregard the destruction of agricultural land through erosion or the removal of moisture-conserving cover until the fertility of the land is irretrievably lost. In many cases it is theoretically possible to observe and learn from the experience of other societies, but effective communication of these experiences appears to be very difficult. There is now enough agricultural knowledge available to enable African nations south of the Sahara to implement procedures that would slow or even stop the southward movement of the desert boundary, but for various social and cultural reasons, the nations seem to be quite unable to take advantage of this information. In other cases, relevant experience is so limited that even specialists have difficulty in deciding among themselves whether or not a trap exists. It is all very well, for example, for computer specialists to extrapolate historical trends in petroleum consumption and announce that if these trends continue our oil resources will quickly be exhausted, but it is quite another matter to assert that adequate energy substitutes will never be found, that the consumption trends will continue as forecast, or even that the arithmetic used in the computations is accurate beyond question. Certainly the homeowner who sets his thermostat at seventy degrees or higher is unlikely to sacrifice his own comfort by "dialing down" to sixty degrees to avert a hypothetical disaster that may never occur and which (except for minor crises) no one has experienced.

Avoiding Time-Delay Traps

It is distressing to see how often time-delay traps are asserted to be nobody's business but the victim's. The super-rationalist model which regards individuals as informed guardians of their own welfare has gained such a hold on our thinking that we often regard entrapped persons as either suffering the deserved consequences of unwarranted stupidity and irrationality or as paying a reasonable and anticipated price for previous pleasures. Thus it is possible for some economists to argue that legal restrictions on cigarette smoking would be improper because the consequences of smoking are well known and smokers can be viewed simply as persons who prefer the pleasure of smoking to longevity. Interference with the decision to take up cigarettes (or drugs, for that matter) would thus amount to an abrogation of a basic right: the freedom to pursue one's own interests, however they may be perceived. Similarly, one occasionally hears assertions that police should forego enforcement of all "victimless crimes" (acts which do no direct harm to outsiders, whatever the consequences may be to the participants themselves), a point of view made the more plausible in that many of the cited examples of victimless crimes do indeed appear to be harmless. Nevertheless, the generalization is based upon a false principle because it is derived from an overoptimistic view of human rationality. We do not believe that people find it easy to stay out of time-delay traps merely because someone has informed them that undesirable consequences lie ahead. Of course, making the entrance to a trap illegal is rarely a satisfactory means for dealing with any situation of this kind, even though, in some cases, it may be one of the few viable mechanisms available.

In the previous chapter, we outlined a series of possible "escapes" from traps. In the following paragraphs, these general principles are applied specifically to time-delay traps.

Consistent with the procedure established already, we will confine ourselves largely to reinterpretations of familiar trap-avoiding behavior, rather than attempting to invent wholly new remedies. Our purpose is to show how the perspective afforded by learning theory enables us to evaluate the effectiveness of various known escapes. The logic of new devices may be clear-cut, yet their effectiveness remains partially speculative in the absence of further empirical experience.

Converting the Trap to a Trade-off

A famous etching by Dürer depicts St. Jerome working in his study faced by a human skull resting on his desk. The skull was not unique to Dürer's particular vision of St. Jerome; the skull was commonly used as a symbol of mortality, hence as a persistent reminder of the brevity of life. Such a device serves as a mechanism for avoiding one time-delay trap—the "wasted-life" trap in which the immediate rewards of excessive materialism or unproductive activity would eventually be followed by regret over a misspent lifetime. Of course, the skull might serve many other functions as well (such as the maintenance of a proper state of humility), and it is intriguing to speculate that, as a deterrent to a time-delay trap, the skull would be effective only for certain personality types. Confronted by such a thing today, one might be led to ponder the futility of doing any work at all, turning instead to outright hedonism.

The use of "reminders" is potentially both a simple and effective way to avoid time-delay traps. Without changing the rewards or punishments, it nevertheless operates to counter the time delay by projecting an image of the punishment into the same time frame as the bait. The individual is thus presented with a choice—a trade-off—rather than a trap. In the St. Jerome example, the temporal transposition of the punishment is merely symbolic. This is probably quite common: in most time-delay traps, it is not possible to reduce or eliminate the time delay itself—to make the hangover coincident with the party, so to speak—but it is often possible to find reminders of or even substantial proxies for future consequences which can be made contemporary with the exposure to the bait of a time-delay trap. Moreover, this is an area in which recent experiments with behavior modification can shed valuable light: empirical evidence strongly supports the view that proxies for future events have a capacity for bridging time lags, so that future consequences of one's actions can be made to influence behavior in the present. It is equally clear from these experiments, however, that the effectiveness of these proxies is heavily dependent upon their tangibility. In this light, the likes of St. Jerome might find an actual skull to afford better protection against the wasted-life trap than, say, written reminders pasted on the wall. A more mundane inference from the same observation is that a homeowner who wishes to induce his son to mow the lawn will do better to reward the son with money now rather than with the promise of a movie three days hence, even though he may know that the money will be used to pay for that same movie. The money, as a tangible representation of the future reward, acquires the reinforcing potential of that reward; since the money itself arrives quickly, the attenuating effect of time delay upon the future movie is eliminated.

Many of the time-delay traps we have been describing could be transformed into trade-offs through the introduction of substantial proxies for future payoffs. In the case of smoking, one could levy a cancer research tax or add special life insurance premiums to the price of each package of cigarettes. Not only could these serve as constant reminders of the future negative consequences in the trap, but the cancer research tax might actually alter the basic structure of the trap by reducing the magnitude of the future punishments. A similar device to apply to traps associated with the exhaustion of our natural resources would be to place a tax on the consumption of such scarce resources, using the revenue to subsidize the search for new supplies or the development of adequate substitutes. In this regard, occasional legislative attempts to hold down petroleum and gas prices may be misdirected, leading us deeper into a trap instead of out of one: instead of transferring a potential future cost of current consumption back into the present, these efforts to drive prices downward conceal the trap and succeed only in convincing most American consumers that the long-run problem does not even exist.

Quite a different technique for transforming traps into trade-offs is demonstrated when proxies for both the behavior and all its consequences are provided simultaneously and in a fashion which can induce appropriate, learned responses to real time-delay situations. We see this as the purpose of stories and parables that teach a moral, particularly in the case of children's stories in which idealized behavior patterns are richly rewarded. To adults, the moralizing in these stories frequently appears forced and the circumstances in which inappropriate behavior is punished are often extravagant and artificial. As trap-avoiding devices, however, they may be quite effective; unlike reality, a story can make the two reinforcers of a trap almost coincident in the telling, and over a fairly short span of real time one can cover the major events of a lifetime. The child's involvement in the story provides strong proxies for the behavior, the near-term pleasure and the future pain. Moreover, such stories can be repeated over and over, reinforcing by proxy trap-avoiding behavior until it becomes so habitual that it carries over into actual practice. Even this book might have some such effect on behavior: our definition of a time-delay situation as a "trap" may have the effect of calling attention to both rewards and punishments simultaneously, and so assist in bridging gaps between the present and the future.

Supplementation and Modification of Existing Reinforcers

A shiny, brand-new automobile is a powerful reward for many American consumers. Rusting fenders, paint blisters, and high maintenance costs are equally powerful punishers. Since rust and engine repairs are inevitable consequences of automobile ownership, the buyer of a new car is a potential victim of the time-delay trap, incurring future punishments for the sake of current gratification. For many buyers, this trap seems to have been modified by a rather extraordinary device: as a part of their campaign to stimulate new car sales, the manufacturers have succeeded in convincing a large part of the public that used cars would be ugly and disreputable even if they were in perfect condition. There is even some evidence that during the late 1950s and 1960s, American automobiles were intentionally designed to lose their appeal after a few years. It was anticipated that the same tailfins which were so glamorous in 1959 would become ludicrous and a source of embarrassment by 1965. So, when the old car begins to rust away and fall apart, that is not really a cause for regret, the loss being tempered by the belief that the thing was unattractive and undesirable anyway.

It is not always possible to neutralize the punishment of a time-delay trap by convincing ourselves that we enjoy our misery, but there do exist traps whose punishment can be readily reduced as a matter of public policy. In the past, sexual promiscuity was frequently followed by venereal diseases, unwanted pregnancies, or both. Now, liberalized abortion laws and the development of antibiotics have greatly reduced the threat from these punishments. Similarly, if an individual enters into marriage for short-term reasons and finds himself or herself suffering long-term unhappiness, our more liberalized divorce laws can greatly reduce the punishment of this trap.

In contrast to these examples, some traps are made worse as a matter of conscious public policy. Perhaps because of an excessive reliance upon a rationalistic view of human behavior, it has become common to attempt to remedy some traps by increasing the punishments rather than reducing them. But when we imprison the drug offender or ostracize the former convict, we add to the (delayed) punishment which already characterizes a trap and so make it an even more serious threat than it was before the "remedy." It can be argued, with some plausibility, that removing such social punishments would serve only to draw more persons into a trap. The threat of imprisonment may tend to reduce drug use, strict divorce laws may lead people to form more carefully considered alliances, and the threat of pregnancy or disease may encourage more stable sexual behavior. On the other hand, all of these punishments are themselves delayed, and, following the principles we have outlined, they consequently have greatly reduced influences over immediate behavior. If a future punishment is to produce present avoidance, then, in order to overcome the effect of the time delay, it might well have to be increased out of all proportion to the problem. Surely there are better ways to inhibit entry into traps than to compound punishments into such massive penalities that they outweigh in severity the problem they are intended to solve. No one would suggest that the solution to the smoking trap is to market cigarettes that produce certain cancer, yet our society's approach to analogous time-delay traps often relies upon such solutions. In general, if social devices are to be used to encourage avoidance of a trap, they will be effective only if they reinforce avoidance through punishment that is coincident with entry into the trap, rather than coincident with the punishments that are already there.

Eliminating the Bait

An ingenious technique for ridding oneself of the smoking habit is to purchase several packages of cigarettes, remove some of the tobacco from each cigarette, insert a little sawdust approximately midway along the length, and then fill each cigarette the rest of the way with the tobacco. One has thereby created a miniature time-delay trap: the enticement of a few satisfying puffs at the beginning of the cigarette is sufficient to begin the smoking, but this is quickly followed by the punishing impact of the sawdust. It is easy to learn to avoid this little trap by avoiding cigarettes themselves; thus the attractiveness of the bait in the larger trap can be effectively neutralized. A more violent form of the same procedure is so-called "aversion therapy" under which consumers who wish to break the smoking habit are subjected to intense unpleasantness through a forced overindulgence of cigarettes. The resulting association of misery with the act of smoking neutralizes the bait thereafter.

The American phenomenon of the diet pill provides another instance of the same approach. The diet pill reduces the immediate pleasures of eating and thus aids in the avoidance of a trap associated with overeating and subsequent obesity. Similarly, methadone avoids a trap by blocking the positively reinforcing properties of heroin. Unfortunately, devices of this sort sometimes replace one trap with another; both diet pills and methadone have been found to have entrapping properties of their own.

It is frustrating to see how often the bait of a time-delay trap is publicly enhanced. Extensive consumer-oriented advertising, promotion of easy payment plans or the services of loan companies, and publicity campaigns stressing the virtues of new models to replace older but serviceable durables all operate to make more attractive the baits in time-delay traps. It is hard enough to save for retirement or schooling for one's children without a barrage of enticement stressing the benefits of immediate consumption. In this regard, television cigarette advertising was particularly repugnant; nevertheless it was many years before we could bring ourselves to remove the commercials from the airwaves. It seems to us that public tolerance for this sort of thing rests largely upon an acceptance of the rationality model rather than a learning model as a reliable predictor of behavior. To the super-rationalist who sees individuals as conscious maximizers of their own long-run interests, advertising can have no impact beyond its information content. According to this view, loan company advertisements only inform us as to funds availability and rates, automobile advertisements simply describe style changes and prices, and cigarette advertisements do nothing more than communicate characteristics of taste and mildness. If such information were all that advertising conveyed, then it would be wholly unobjectionable. While we by no means reject the view that some advertising is essentially informative, this general attitude appears, from the perspective of learning theory, to be extremely naive and likely to generate a comfortable tolerance of forces that encourage entry into many dangerous traps.

Adding Punishment to the Bait

Alcoholics Anonymous has developed an elaborate procedure for assisting its members to avoid drinking. In general, the method provides positive reinforcements for the "act" of *not* drinking, although the reinforcers used frequently have nothing to do with alcohol itself but rely instead upon the encouragement and support of friendly fellow members. Under such circumstances, the rewards associated with alcohol are unaffected, but a new element has been added to the situation. Taking the bait amounts to a betrayal of the trust, support, and encouragement received from other people. Thus the trap may be avoided, not because the basic reinforcers in the alcoholic's trap have been altered, but because a new negative reinforcer competes with the bait, thus reinforcing untrapped behavior.

To be effective, it is important that the new punishment occur close in time to the bait. Parents frequently attempt to inhibit the indulgence in cigarettes, alcohol, or drugs on the part of their offspring by tying punishments to the bait, but often the punishments are ineffective because they are themselves delayed. Almost everyone has heard of some parent who has offered his children a sum of money—one hundred or one thousand dollars or even more—if they will refrain from smoking or drinking until reaching a specified age such as eighteen or twenty-one. Such offers are intended to associate economic losses with the act of taking up cigarettes or drinking, but it is clear that the losses are not, in fact, coincident with the behavior they are intended to discourage. Since the promised reward cannot be received until a specified age, such offers serve only to increase the *future* punishment associated with the habit. The boy who begins to smoke at age fifteen hardly suffers at all from the loss of the money he was to receive six years hence. Having never received the reward, its sacrifice is easily borne. In the case of intelligent and strong-willed offspring who are sensitive to the future consequences of present-day actions, the proposal of a future reward may successfully inhibit the acquisition of a smoking habit (although for such persons this added disincentive is probably quite unnecessary); for others, the procedure only succeeds in compounding the trap, in worsening the future outcome without operating at all in the time frame in which the bait presents itself. To our way of thinking, a similar but much more effective device would be to give one's offspring the reward now, perhaps deposited in a savings account, with the condition that the money and accumulated interest be returned to its donor immediately should the undesired habit ever be indulged. In this way, the bait in the trap is associated with a simultaneous financial loss. From a practical economic standpoint the two procedures may appear to be identical, but from the reinforcement point of view they are worlds apart.

Potentially, all time-delay traps may be avoided by superimposing new punishments to compete with the existing reinforcers, but experience suggests that this method is not as effective as others. In the first place, there is the ever-present danger that the new punishment will fail to be concurrent with the bait in a trap and instead will occur later. Second, even if the new negative reinforcer is concurrent with the bait, it may not be adequate to ensure avoidance of the trap, and we have then added a gratuitous punishment to an already unpleasant situation. In either case the overall well-being of those who are trapped is made worse. This result is noticeably obvious in the various attempts that have been made from time to time to block entry into traps by legal means. Legal processes are proverbially slow, and the sanctions the law may eventually impose can be delayed even more than the punishment that is already a part of the trap. Because of their tardiness, legal punishments, if they are to work at all, must be disproportionately severe in order to have potential for bridging the time delay. Moreover, it often seems to be the case that what is defined as "unlawful" behavior is not taking the bait but being in the trap. A man is not arrested for taking a drink, but he may very well be arrested for being drunk. Similarly, people are not lawbreakers for borrowing too much money, but only for failing to pay it back. For all of these reasons, the devised punishments often are both excessive and ineffective. In making drug possession illegal, we have added the risk of imprisonment to the risks already associated with drug use, and since the punishment is remote, it seems to have had little effect. Until recently, for instance, in many states, marijuana possession was punishable by several years in a state penitentiary—surely a devastating experience to most who were convicted—yet we have no reason to believe that this had any deterrent effect. Instead it may have compounded the trap by offering an opportunity for young people to demonstrate their fearlessness before their contemporaries—consuming drugs not only for their physiological effects but also to gain peer-group acceptance.

Trap Insurance

As an alternative to promoting trap avoidance through the imposition of new penalties that reduce the attractiveness of the bait, one might use new rewards to reduce the punishments in existing traps, so as to ease the discomfort suffered by their victims. This we see to be the function of old-age assistance programs that reduce the burdens of those who have failed to save enough to sustain themselves after they are too old to work and Aid to Dependent Children programs that protect, in some degree, those who have borne children in an unstable family situation. These are, in effect, social insurance programs that compensate those who have fallen into time-delay traps.

It is obvious that such insurance programs provide a solution to social traps only in the limited sense that their victims do not suffer as much as they would if their loss were not spread out over the wider society. Since nothing is done to modify the basic rewards and punishments that characterize the traps, their incidence and hence their social costs are not really reduced. Indeed, many people recognize that social insurance programs exacerbate the problems they are supposed to relieve. By offsetting punishments that would ordinarily induce avoidance, the trap may be entered more readily than ever. This effect is, of course, reduced by the same time-delay mechanism: the insurance benefits are coincident with the delayed punishments, and a person who is trapped because the future has too little influence over current behavior may be no more likely to be swayed by future rewards than by future punishments. On the other hand, every social insurance program must confront the possibility that there exist individuals for whom the insurance benefits are sufficient to transform what would formerly have been recognized as trapped behavior into a viable way of life. Social insurance protects those who would be trapped in any case, but subverts those who otherwise might have found their own means of escape.

Reinforcing Competing Behaviors

Sir Arthur Conan Doyle had Sherlock Holmes turn to cocaine whenever his primary occupation as private investigator entered into a period of slack. The behavioral description was apt: indulgence in drugs constitutes a tacit admission that one has nothing better to do with one's time. There are, after all, countless activities that are incompatible with drug taking and which have their own rewarding consequences. Anyone familiar with learning behavior would agree that the restoration of these reinforcements, placing them in competition with the rewards of drug taking, would provide a promising solution to contemporary drug problems.

It is usually quite easy to find examples of activities that are interfered with or even made impossible when one enters a time-delay trap. For example, drugs interfere with effective performance in school or at a job, and so it is only when such goals lose their rewarding properties that indulgence becomes a tempting alternative. In effect, drugs no longer conflict with anything that matters. Alcohol traps operate similarly, consumption depending upon the personal importance of competing and incompatible behavior and the extent to which alcohol causes interference. Before a concert, a professional violinist or pianist will reject the offer of even a glass of beer because it takes very little alcohol to produce a dramatic reduction in manual dexterity and concentration, whereas a Madison Avenue advertising executive may think nothing of having three martinis at lunch, evidently because the alcohol interferes very little with whatever it is that he does in the afternoon.

Rewarding alternatives that are incompatible with an unwanted habit is common in the list of techniques people employ when they attempt to give up cigarettes. Smokers have been known to chew gum, suck on straws, smoke pipes, or eat heavily—all behaviors that interfere physically with the act of smoking. It appears to be an unfortunate fact of life that, except possibly for eating, none of these is a sufficiently powerful reinforcer to guarantee success. Certainly the difficulty in giving up smoking is in part attributable to the apparent lack of sufficiently reinforcing behaviors which are incompatible with smoking itself.

Instead of reinforcing new kinds of behavior, some methods of avoiding traps seem designed to establish links between trap-avoiding behavior and established activities that are already rewarded. During the 1960s, economists marveled at the rapid growth of "Christmas clubs"—personal savings accounts built up over one year's time and then paid out at Christmas. Banks paid little or no interest on these accounts and economists could not understand why people would use them instead of ordinary savings accounts which pay interest and can be accumulated and dissipated along the same seasonal patterns as a Christmas club, if the depositor so desires. What conflicts with a rational model of behavior, however, fits neatly into a psychological one. The Christmas club imposes an automatic and routine collection system that demands (and reinforces) monthly deposits from members. The act of saving money already enjoys substantial cultural rewards and the Christmas club exploits this fact to encourage avoidance of a time-delay trap—the failure to prepare in advance for a heavy, seasonal financial drain. It is an important fact that people join Christmas clubs voluntarily; the choice (over ordinary savings deposits) reflects a recognition on the part of members that they need these periodic reinforcements; otherwise they are in a trap from which they cannot easily escape by themselves.

In its broadest sense, education is a technique for establishing and encouraging new forms of behavior through expansion in the reinforcement systems available to any individual. By this we mean more than the obvious examples of music, art, or literature courses which stimulate a student's sensitivities to the extent that the aesthetic contents of these disciplines come to afford more pleasure than they did previously. Of greater importance is the stimulation of intellectual and interpersonal responses that govern all adult activities, making enough of them sufficiently satisfying to preclude traps. In addition, the educational arena is the natural one wherein we establish and reinforce all kinds of trap-avoiding rules of thumb. Through the proxies for personal experience provided by schooling, one may be encouraged to prepare for future responsibilities, to be wary of the unforeseen consequences of cigarettes and drugs, and even to make routine six-month trips to the dentist. None of these educational functions come about through reliance upon knowledge alone. To be informed that heavy smoking may cause cancer is no more likely to forestall one's first experiment with a cigarette than the knowledge that Chopin wrote beautiful music is likely to encourage a seven year old to practice piano scales. From a psychological point of view, intellectual information is largely incidental to behavior determination; if we wish to make use of the potential of education for encouraging trap-avoiding behavior, we must recognize that rewards and punishments have to be made concrete. In a sense, we are all from Missouri: seeing (and touching and experiencing) is believing, and mere descriptions of the elements of a trap cannot contribute much toward its avoidance. Facts, by themselves, do not reinforce anything.

Superordinate Authority

In practice, many traps seem to be avoided by delegating the relevant decision-making power to someone who is not subject to the entrapping reinforcers. To be effective, the transfer of decision power must be irrevocable, at least in the short run, and so most devices in this class must have the force of law. For example, the majority of employers in the United States are required to make various deductions from their employees' salaries. The deductions include contributions to the social security program, federal income tax obligations, and payments for health insurance programs—all of which help to avoid potentially serious time-delay traps. The social security contribution provides some protection against overconsumption in the present and consequential destitution after retirement, the federal income tax withholding protects from overconsumption during the year followed by a disastrous income tax obligation on April 15, and the health insurance protects us against lack of financial preparedness for the risk of extensive illness. In a similar vein, we require our children to attend school until age sixteen, we forbid the sale of alcohol to minors, and we have outlawed the nonprescription sale of hard drugs to anyone in an attempt to deprive ourselves (and other people as well) of the wherewithal to enter traps.

We have already commented upon one major weakness of this method: legal devices have a tendency to compound traps rather than solve them, especially because of the delayed punishment they administer to those who are already victims. If legal sanctions are to induce avoidance despite the time delay inherent in them, they must be expanded out of all reasonable proportion to the crime they are to inhibit. It is often the case that legal methods for preventing trapped behavior also create profitable opportunities for those who habitually flaunt the law anyway, thus providing some of the least desirable segments of our society with valuable economic encouragement. In effect, outlawing certain behaviors creates a black market which increases the rewards for those willing to take the risk of providing illegal commodities or services. Marijuana, a hardy weed, might be cheaper than tobacco if it were legal, and the sizable profits going to those who traffic in the drug would be eliminated.

An additional objection to this use of superordinate authority is that the legal system necessarily affects individuals who are not trapped, as well as those who are, and this can impose unnecessary constraints. Some people feel that social security is not a very good investment and believe that they could do better on their own. If we did our own tax withholding we could at least gain interest from savings banks on our withholding deposits over the year. Prohibition attempted to deprive moderate and light drinkers of a harmless and enjoyable indulgence at the same time that it protected others from their excesses. In the latter case, it is even probable that the accumulated costs which Prohibition imposed upon those who were not trapped exceeded the benefits that were gained by the rescue (or at least partial rescue, given the frequency of violations) of those who were trapped. Undoubtedly this fact contributed to Prohibition's subsequent repeal. In general, we believe that mechanisms which permit individuals to recognize traps and associate themselves voluntarily with alternative patterns of behavior are preferable to the systems that impose, at least in part, the burdens of trap-avoidance devices onto those who had successfully stayed free on their own.

4 *Ignorance Traps*

A Rake's Progress
(detail of Plate III)

William Hogarth
engraving 1735

An eighteenth-century
morality tale of the
ruin of a young
nobleman, enticed to
his destruction by
drink, gambling, and
fast women.

It is common for those who first encounter modern theories of reinforcement learning to view with distaste the implication that even goal-oriented human behavior is essentially myopic. Our capacity for analysis and foresight as well as our general intelligence provides us with a self-perception that is difficult to reconcile with a model of behavior which emphasizes our susceptibility to the immediate rewards and punishments that happen to impinge upon us. In fact, psychologists are by no means in agreement as to the extent of the myopia which they themselves are willing to attribute to human beings in learning situations.

Temporal myopia, although a marked deviation from rationality, is the most widely accepted of the deficiencies attributable to the reinforcement process, and it is, of course, the mechanism which produces our time-delay trap. However, there are other forms of behavioral myopia, not based upon time lags, which also enjoy a great deal of experimental and anecdotal support. Several of these are so at variance with analytical or rational models of behavior that we have grouped them together, characterizing them as "ignorance" traps.

One of the most interesting discoveries to come out of the research on learning is that rewards seem to lose very little of their effectiveness when they accompany a particular behavior only some of the time. Indeed, if a particular action is followed sometimes by a reward and sometimes by nothing, the intensity of behavioral effort that can be induced seems to be out of all proportion to the benefits which the cumulative rewards confer. Moreover, if the rewards were to cease entirely, the behavior upon which they were contingent will persist far longer than if the rewards had occurred regularly during the learning process. This property does not necessarily imply irrationality, because a complete termination of reward is not easily recognized when each occurrence of the reward itself is unpredictable. Suppose that a long series of plays on a slot machine fails to produce a win; how is one to distinguish a machine that is programmed to pay nothing from a run of bad luck? It is possible that the persistence of learned behavior following an intermittent reward pattern merely reflects lack of information regarding the change in reward likelihood. This view is given support by evidence that the persistence of the learned behavior in the absence of rewards is greatest when the reward is eliminated through a gradual reduction in its frequency, rather than abruptly terminated. Notwithstanding such cognitive explanations, the behavior induced by intermittent rewards appears excessively persistent by any reasonable standard. Through careful and gradual reduction in the frequency of reward, a pigeon can be induced to peck continually at a target, receiving a reward (a pellet of food) only once in thousands of pecks, until the bird actually collapses, exhausted from this fruitless exertion.

That humans, too, are trapped by intermittent reward situations is obvious from the variety and popularity of gambling games. Statistically, when one plays "against the house," all gambling is eventually a losing proposition. Although some might argue that the inevitable financial loss is outweighed by the pleasure and excitement of the activity, the set features of the compulsive gambler at the tables suggest that often something quite unpleasant is taking place. The human in the gambling trap, like the pigeon in the intermittent reward experiment, may well exhaust his resources in an effort destined to end in defeat. To nongamblers, the predicament of the victim in such a trap appears to be absurd and unnecessary. The laws of probability that underlie all gambles are well known and, though subtle in some respects, they are surely well enough understood to prevent disastrous entrapment. The gambling trap arises from ignorance which could be dispelled by the rational acceptance of a few well-known properties of random phenomena.

Superstition provides another dimension to the ignorance trap. Since learning takes place through the simple association of paired events, a particular action closely followed by a reward is likely to be repeated whether or not any objective or causal relation exists between the behavior and the reward. What is surprising in human behavior is that this sort of incidental learning occurs even when the likelihood of a genuine connection between the behavior and the reward is extremely remote. Sports writers often make much of the superstition of professional athletes and delight in the ritualistic behavior of baseball players. In 1976, the Detroit Tigers' pitching sensation, Mark "The Bird" Fidrych, was idolized by baseball writers not only for his athletic ability, but equally for his ritualistic habits: getting on his hands and knees before each inning and smoothing the dirt around the pitching mound, and then pleading, cajoling, and scolding his baseball before each pitch. In terms of the learning process, it is easy to understand how such behavior develops. A baseball pitcher may feel an itch, scratch his side, and then, coincidentally, throw a perfect strike. The likelihood of scratching his side again before the next pitch, whether it itches or not, is increased by the close temporal proximity between the act of scratching and the successful pitch. If it should happen that the following two, three, or four pitches are equally successful, the scratching behavior may become a permanent feature of the pitching routine. Eventually, the routine may develop into quite a long series of such incidentally reinforced activities: the pitcher kicks dirt on the mound, rubs his hands, spits, looks to first, looks at his feet, touches his side, pulls his cap, rubs his stomach, eyes the batter, looks again to first, and throws, each of these actions carried out in strict ritualistic perfection. From a scientific point of view, only a few of these activities are functional; one cannot easily rationalize the existence of any causal connections between scratching, spitting, or rubbing and successful pitching. Indeed, the lack of any connection at all (scratching does no harm just as it does no good) implies that we are describing what appears to be an intermittent reward situation: pitches are sometimes successful and sometimes not, but if every pitch is preceded by a scratch, then there are ample instances in which the necessary reinforcement will take place. According to the principles already described, the random element in this process will have the effect of increasing the persistence of the learned behavior, because a nonoccurrence of reward is no evidence that the reward is totally unconnected to the behavior. Imagine our pitcher's reaction to a string of bad pitches, each of which was preceded by the necessary scratch. If previously he had thrown a perfect pitch every time he scratched his side, then the string of bad pitches could be taken to be evidence that scratching does not produce successful pitches. If, occasionally, a bad pitch has followed the act of scratching, then the string of bad throws does not constitute any such refutation because the proposition now is that scratching one's side only increases the likelihood of perfect pitches, rather than making them inevitable.

We have characterized reinforcement learning as a method for finding one's way about in a world that is too subtle and too complicated to permit analysis of all the consequences of one's behavior. From this standpoint, what we are calling superstitious behavior is not necessarily undesirable; it may lead us to stumble upon genuinely beneficial behaviors. The primitive farmer may have no notion why a fish planted alongside his seed leads to a more healthy growth of his crop or why rotating crops improves production, but the association that occurs between crop rotation and fertilization on the one hand, and bountiful crops on the other is sufficiently clear to reward and sustain effective agricultural habits. Of course, many other associations are likely to occur at the same time, and, as in the case of our baseball pitcher, the agricultural ritual that develops may include a number of activities which are not defensible on any scientific grounds, as the farmer praises his gods, plants his seeds, sacrifices fish alongside the seeds, performs a dance, and prays for rain.

The role of intermittent rewards and of chance associations in shaping behavior are widely accepted among psychologists today, and a good deal of data has been accumulated concerning the nature of the connection. Other forms of ignorance traps exist, although far less documentary evidence for them is available. For example, it seems to be possible for very intense rewards (or the anticipation thereof) to blind some people to even relatively obvious punishments. In most of these cases, the punishment is delayed, but unlike time-delay traps, the victim is unaware of, or ignores, the punishments which lie ahead. In the time-delay situation, the punishment is recognized by the victim, but its impact is underweighted or discounted. In the case of an ignorance trap, a punishment goes entirely unrecognized, even though its magnitude may be more than sufficient to overcome any time delay involved. Our culture is replete with examples of formal "cooling off" or waiting periods that appear to be intended to give potential ignorance-trap victims enough time to reflect upon the total consequences of their contemplated actions. Long engagements (and even a three-day wait for a license) may avert some impulsive and subsequently disastrous marriages; novitiates in religious orders must wait several years before being allowed to make the formal commitment to permanent membership; some recent consumer protection legislation allows for a grace period during which a purchaser can reconsider and possibly revoke a contractual agreement; and even the 1948 Taft-Hartley Act allows the president to impose a sixty-day cooling-off period upon management and labor in an attempt to avert hot-tempered commitments by both sides to irreconcilable positions.

Given the natural admiration and respect for rational action that we all possess, it is not surprising that the victims of ignorance traps so often succeed in devising plausible theories which are used to justify their actions. Our baseball pitcher may speculate that some physiological connection exists between side-scratching and pitching and use the resulting theory to "explain" behavior that otherwise might appear ridiculous. He may even write a book about it. In the same vein, the primitive farmer may develop a theology which will give a purpose to his prayers and fish-planting and justify his otherwise superfluous ritual dances. Even the overeager purchaser who comes to regret a hasty contract can stress his lack of information in explaining a bad decision. Some psychologists describe the general process of rationalizing behavior as a "dissonance" reduction, which arises from a need to reduce an uncomfortable conflict between what we do and what we perceive to be appropriate behavior. Thus we are often inclined to ignore any evidence that suggests that what we have chosen to do is not the best of all the choices available to us. What is important for our purposes is finding that these rationalizations do take place, and that dissonance reduction is itself rewarding. Hence any world view which successfully justifies learned behavior will itself be strongly encouraged. Broadly speaking, any theory used to eliminate an incompatibility between rationality and actual behavior is rewarded, and thus the rewards that originally reinforced only one specific behavior are now, indirectly, reinforcing a theory as well.

It is a property of all theories that they can be applied to circumstances other than those upon which they were originally based. The same theology that a farmer applies to the growing of corn can be used in other agricultural pursuits. A sufficiently inventive baseball pitcher may develop a theory of muscular control which he extends to entirely unrelated sports. Through this process of generalization, the simple myopia that led to an original ignorance trap may be applied to a whole range of new situations. What might have been a trivial punishment in the simple ignorance trap now becomes multiplied into a series of punishments. This process of extension through theory is familiar to those who engage in scientific research. In order to make headway with any scientific problem, a researcher must simplify his view of things, presuming for the purposes of his analysis that certain relationships among his variables are unimportant or perhaps nonexistent. If he formulates a theory that deals successfully with a number of previously unexplained phenomena, the scientist himself has been rewarded in the application of his theory and in the use of the assumptions on which it rested. When new problems arise in similar or related fields, or when entirely new phenomena are discovered, the scientist naturally attempts to apply the same theory, even though there may be no substantial evidence supporting the appropriateness of such an application. While there is nothing in principle wrong with such a procedure, it is evident that a theory, once rewarded through a few successful applications, can acquire a powerful hold over its adherents. If his theory is found to be inadequate to explain some newly discovered phenomenon, our scientist may respond to the new information not by rejecting his theory, but by rejecting the data as unimportant or erroneously gathered, or he might develop elaborate rationalizations through entirely speculative subtheories to bring the data and the theory into agreement. Indeed, the development of formal theories of behavior based upon rationality seems to have followed just such a pattern. We would expect the learning mechanism to be effective in bringing about "good" behavior patterns in most static (simultaneous reinforcer) situations, and it is therefore no surprise that under such circumstances, models of rational behavior would be able to predict with considerable accuracy. This success, however, has led many social scientists to attempt to extend the same principles much further, and this has required the invention of new appendages for the theory, such as time discounting or the use of elaborate statistical methods for dealing with uncertainty. These modifications carry the analyses into much more complicated areas in which the plausibility of the necessary assumptions is, at best, very remote. Of course, any well-trained scientist is generally expected to be sensitive to the possible inadequacies of his theories; even so, the tenacity with which most adhere to their established views is impressive and amply demonstrates the extent to which theories can become established through the rewards they produce.

Another ignorance trap which is frequently generalized through theory is found among gamblers. We have already noted that intermittent rewards can sustain behavior which incurs costs far greater than can be justified by the magnitude of the rewards themselves; as an example, we described the gambler who is periodically rewarded but who fails to apply the laws of probability which could reveal to him that over the long run he is making a mistake. This might be called naive gambling, where only the *action* of placing a bet (putting a coin in a slot machine) is rewarded. Theory, however, usually plays a prominent part in the rationalizations of gamblers, and so this elementary process is usually elaborated into some form of sophisticated gambling. The sophisticated gambler does not merely pour money down a slot machine or place his bets randomly on a roulette wheel; he has developed a "system" which reflects a theory about the laws of nature. Some such systems are widely accepted by gamblers and nongamblers alike. The most common employ one form or another of the so-called gamblers' fallacy. As an example, suppose that a coin known to be "fair" has been flipped ten times and has come up heads every time. The gambler might now appeal to the "Law of Averages" for the (erroneous) prediction that the probability of tails is very high on the next toss. In a sense, the coin "owes" us a tail. If the coin is tossed again and does come up tails, the theory appears substantiated; the gambler wins and enjoys the additional gratification of having demonstrated his superior insight. Naturally, the future application of the theory is made more likely. If this theory is applied whenever a string of heads or tails occurs, then statistically it will be vindicated fifty percent of the time and, as an intermittent reward, this vindication occurs quite often enough for the theory to become firmly implanted in the gambler's repertoire of behavior. That this should happen is wholly illogical, but as a practical matter it is an everyday experience. In any situation governed by the laws of probability, predictions of specific outcomes are bound to prove to be correct some fraction of the time; thus the rules which generated those predictions are periodically reinforced. In consequence, there is considerable potential for intermittent rewards to shape behavior in ways which produce ignorance traps, since it is not only the isolated behavior—the specific bet—which is reinforced, but also the use of the rule. If the rule is false, then all behavior guided by it can lead one into ignorance traps.

The sophisticated gambler's theory usually applies only to repeated instances of a given event, such as the flip of a coin, roll of a die, or spin of a wheel. Most theories, whether casually developed world views or elaborately formal scientific models, are meant to describe both repetitions of events already experienced and events occurring under similar, though not identical, circumstances. Moreover, it is often the theory itself which defines when circumstances are sufficiently similar to justify its application. This capacity of a theory to define its scope of application can lead into an ignorance trap even if the originally learned behavior does not involve a trap at all. For example, most of us have learned from our own experience that successful family budgeting requires, over the long run, that our expenditures must not exceed our income. Temporary excesses and large purchases may be covered by loans, but since debts must be paid off, eventually the excess expenditure must be paid for and the long-run budget balanced. The same is true of a business, in that a continuing excess of expenditure over revenues must ultimately lead to financial disaster. It is not uncommon for these simple, learned "facts of life" to be extended to a wholly new area—the federal budget—in support of an advocacy of balance between federal revenues and expenditures. However, this is not really a valid extension; at the very least, the taxing power of the government adds an entirely new dimension to the situation. Economists point out that a routinely balanced budget is not a guarantee of prosperity and many argue that it may, in fact, lead to wholesale unemployment and economic depression. The dedicated supporter of balanced federal budgets may be in an ignorance trap produced by the inappropriate extension of a valid rule. (One must be careful here: the economists' arguments are themselves the products of complicated learning experiences, and support for budget imbalances may also reflect a trap!)

Ritualistic behavior occurs as the consequence of incidental associations between actions and the rewards that happen to follow. The theory that is likely to be developed to accompany the ritual may develop into a theology given widespread applications in all sorts of other, unrelated circumstances. Since theories usually define the areas of their own relevance, those which become theologies may aspire to application of unlimited breadth. The powerful resistance met by the Copernican view of the sun as the center of our planetary system was not due to any social concern about the movement of planets and stars. The antagonism arose because, as an incidental by-product of the theology then current, the domain of man had been taken to be placed at the center of the universe; the Copernican theory appeared to be in open conflict with this rather peripheral application of contemporary faith. Apart from navigational uses, the behavior of the planets was of no great practical concern to anyone, but by challenging the validity of this extension, Copernicus, in effect, challenged the whole religious and philosophical structure of his society. It is little wonder that he was so vehemently opposed. With respect to their understanding of the solar system, Copernicus's contemporaries were in a trap, forced to accept a particular physical thesis only because of an unnecessary extension of a theory which applied elsewhere.

Theories may be adhered to for either of two reasons: they may have been validated by situations in which causes were followed, at least occasionally, by the expected or predicted effects, or adherence to a particular theory may be rewarding in its own right, quite apart from empirical validity. If Professor John Smith develops a theory subsequently named the "Smith hypothesis" by his admiring colleagues, he is likely to be among the last to recognize any evidence that his model, in fact, has no empirical relevance. Indeed, it is a common observation (in the social sciences particularly) that outmoded theories rarely die before their original proponents die. Nonscientists are equally susceptible to attractive theories. In the seventeenth and eighteenth centuries in England, for example, it was considered to be criminal for any member of the lower classes to permit his financial obligations to exceed his ability to pay them off. This attitude probably gained some support from the consideration of the harm such a person does to his creditors who, in good faith, gave him the use of their resources. But surely it was strengthened by its implication of moral rectitude on the part of those who stayed solvent. The result was a trap: debtors, as criminals, had to be imprisoned, thus depriving both debtor and creditor of the opportunity to recover their losses. Perhaps the contemporary view that the victims of drug traps are criminals has a similar explanation.

Ways Out

Nothing can be more frustrating to the believer in human rationality than the utter failure of common sense arguments in drawing victims out of traps. "But can't you see that smoking (or drinking, or gambling) will destroy you?" goes the refrain of one who can see the punishment from which he may wish to save a trapped friend. It is their conflict with common sense which makes all social traps troublesome and, incidentally, it is the fact that trapped behavior persists in the face of its irrationality that provides some of the most convincing evidence that reinforcement learning plays a central part in establishing the behavioral habits of each of us.

It seems that the conflict with rationality is most apparent, and the exasperation of nonvictims with less fortunate acquaintances most pronounced, in the case of ignorance traps. Not only may the victim of one of these traps fail to acknowledge the validity of demonstrations that his behavior is unreasonable; he may even have gone on to develop a firmly held theory of his own which completely justifies his behavior by making it appear rational. The gambler's system is, in his mind, as good a model of the world as the scientist's naive belief that some events in nature are random. Thus the theory which has been devised to justify superstitious behavior becomes an "insight" at or beyond the frontiers of conventional knowledge, rather than a simple contradiction to ordinary common sense. Such rationalizations can lead to full-blown tragedies. To take one example, most human illnesses are overcome by the body's own defense mechanisms and even the most serious diseases occasionally disappear. If these events happen to be associated with behavior that does not involve, or even actively rejects, medical treatment, an ignorance trap can develop in which potentially beneficial medical care is never used, even when it is genuinely necessary. The associated theories frequently include assertions that those who deliver medical care are either foolish or corrupt. Thus people who replace orthodox treatments for cancer with Laetrile often defend their actions with the assertion that doctors are ignorant, or even that the medical community is deliberately suppressing evidence of its effectiveness because the conventional treatments are so much more profitable. Other cases involve those theories which provide rewards to their subscribers because of their adherence, alone. Examples include beliefs in "racial superiority" held by such groups as the Ku Klux Klan and the Nazi party. Since the adherents of racial superiority theories invariably include themselves in the superior class, factual material disproving such theories is resisted for the psychological reason that the theory itself is reinforcing.

The point is that escape from ignorance traps is particularly difficult since the victims may see no compelling reason for changing their behavior. In other sorts of traps there are usually moments when people can recognize glimmerings of the predicaments they are in: heavy smokers occasionally wish they could break the habit; drug addicts may long for freedom; and certainly commuters trapped in massive traffic jams must sometimes reflect upon the possibility that there is a better way to organize things. The presence of such uneasiness with the way things are may mean that if effective escapes are made available they will be taken up, voluntarily, as people attempt to extricate themselves from unpleasant situations. Ignorance traps, on the other hand, are characterized by the failure of their victims to appreciate their dilemmas at all. Even the habitual gambler, who might be expected to reflect upon his situation after a large loss, is apparently more likely to modify his system in an attempt to correct a flaw than he is to question the reasonableness of his entire pattern of behavior. The smoker warns others away from his trap, but gamblers never cease to invite others in. A consequence of this characteristic of ignorance traps is that attempts to avoid them or help others out often leads to conflict. If many people believe that their own particular race is inherently superior, then those who see that belief as a social trap will face opposition which is much more intense than is found in an ordinary debate. Even those with the best of motives may then find themselves abandoning reasoned persuasion and instead advocating coercion or the use of some superordinate authority to impose what they see as untrapped behavior upon an obstinate population. The habitual use of coercion, however, may compound our problems because it is as readily applied to situations in which one has wrongly analyzed a trap as to situations in which a trap really operates. Furthermore, coercion inevitably engenders conflict, which produces more traps in its own right. In describing possible escapes, we wish to focus first upon voluntary means for escaping traps before turning to higher authority to impose solutions to our problems.

Converting the Trap to a Trade-off

A slot machine is designed to operate so that when it is fed silver dollars it will return nothing on most occasions, a few dollars on some other occasions, and a very large number of dollars on rare occasions. Suppose that we kept records over several years and discovered that the total payout of this machine equalled $8,000 for every $10,000 deposited. We might then produce a new machine which returned three quarters and a nickel on each occasion that a dollar was deposited and argue that the economics of the two machines were identical: each would pay out $8,000 for every $10,000 deposited. But, despite the objective equivalence of the two situations, it is unlikely that we can find anyone to play our new slot machine. Some would refuse, saying the "fun" had gone out of it; to those who disbelieve the laws of probability, the substantive situation has changed and the opportunity to make a killing has been lost; to the psychologist, the peculiarly powerful influence of random and intermittent rewards has been eliminated by the substitution of a routine and regular reward system. Rewording this last view, the trap has been converted into a trade-off and rational behavior has replaced superstitious behavior.

There are alternative methods of getting this result; instead of modifying the slot machine, we could sell an insurance policy to the gambler. Premiums would be charged against his winnings and benefits would be paid to cover his losses. In order to break even, however, the insurance company would be forced to collect all winnings above eighty cents in order to have sufficient income to protect the policy holder against only 80 percent of his losses. Again, the gambler is left with exactly eighty cents returned for every dollar deposited. The conclusion is the same as before: if the gambler were required to hold such a policy, gambling would cease.

It might make for good social policy to experiment with insurance schemes that would protect gamblers against extreme losses. Even in a case which only approximated the payoffs of the modified slot machine, the underlying trade-off which characterizes gambling would be made more explicit because premium charges could be levied against every gamble. The sad fact is, however, that there seems to be very little interest or social concern with inhibiting the action of the gambling trap. Instead, through lotteries, race tracks, and other forms of legalized gambling, state governments have found it profitable to manipulate this trap so as to supplement their own revenues, in effect exploiting those who are already victims. We believe that this is another instance in which general acceptance of the rationalist model of behavior has led to a tolerant acceptance of a damaging trap. Apparently, the dominant social attitude toward gambling is that it is only slightly immoral. This belief has enabled governments to raise revenues on the questionable grounds that it is more justifiable to tax immoral than moral activities. If such taxes were intended to inhibit gambling, then we might treat them as methods for encouraging avoidance—adding punishments so as to diminish the attractiveness of the bait of a trap—but, once a state is in a position to profit from gambling, it hawks its lottery like

any common tout and becomes an agent of further entrapment. If one believes that gambling is merely a disreputable
activity that remains under the rational control of the gambler,
such policies may be supportable; but if one accepts the view
that intermittent reinforcement can encourage trapped behavior, then these policies are reprehensible in that they amount
to the further exploitation of those who have already demonstrated their inability to protect their own interests.

Supplementation and Modification of Existing Reinforcers

A teenager who speeds along the highway at eighty-five miles
an hour may be in an ignorance trap. The exhilaration and
sense of superiority over other, slower drivers are powerfully
reinforcing, and the driver, like many other victims of these
traps, has a theory: it is that his youthful skill will protect him
from accidents. If he does have an accident, his injuries are
very likely to have been reduced if he was wearing a seat belt
or if his automobile was engineered to protect its occupants
from collisions. In effect, through public opinion and legal
pressures, steps have been taken to reduce the severity of punishment in this trap, making it a less serious threat to those
who fall victim to it.

Similar measures could be taken to combat gambling traps.
If state and local governments were less interested in profiteer-
ing, they might consider the legalization of state gambling
programs that would offer "fair" odds, perhaps even with a
built-in insurance program designed to protect individuals
against impoverishment as a consequence of a very long string
of losses. Such an alternative would be preferred by bettors to
competing forms of gambling, because once the profits to
sponsors had been eliminated, it would be possible to offer
the same pattern of prizes at a much lower cost per bet. There
would still be victims of gambling traps, but as a group their
losses would be much smaller.

Eliminating the Bait

In the final analysis, the bait in an ignorance trap is the erroneous association between an action and a reward, and any procedure which breaks the connection will successfully defeat the trap. This form of remedy is made particularly difficult, however, by the fact that sooner or later most victims of ignorance traps manage to invent theories that justify, rationalize, and even generalize these associations. The gambler develops his system, the superstitious athlete evolves some theory of muscle tone, the primitive farmer establishes his theology, and so on. To disarm the ignorance trap it becomes necessary to replace these theories with equally plausible (and perhaps even more accurate) substitutes. This is especially necessary when the false theory itself is rewarded, as when the gambler has his system occasionally "vindicated" by a random win, or the advocate of imprisonment for drug offenders is reassured of his own invulnerability to addiction and consequently his moral superiority.

The classroom is the obvious place to begin the process of developing trap-avoiding theories, but formal education is completed too soon to provide continuing effective defenses against the variety of traps that arise later. Outside of the classroom, contemporary science is surprisingly ill-adapted to accomplish the revision of commonly held false theories. It is not only that the scientific demonstration of natural relationships typically takes place at a highly abstract level, requiring the understanding of analytical techniques that are beyond the experience of most people, but it is also that the scientific community is so often jealous of its private abstractions: there is so much personal gratification to be gained from the use of a language that is accessible only to a chosen elite that there is reluctance to convert scientific insights into everyday terms. Therefore, the elderly lady at the slot machine is not likely to be impressed by what is, to her, a lot of mathematical gibberish and which apparently does not even address itself to her conviction that soon she will get her big win. Moreover, many attempts to demonstrate the inaccuracy of some popularly held theories focus only upon the erroneous models without presenting convincing alternatives. Unfortunately, this is unavoidable in some cases because the scientific models themselves are essentially negative. The specialist in probability theory maintains that the roll of a die is governed only by the laws of chance and not by a more determinate process. This is not a positive proposition which he can "prove," however, but only an inference drawn from the absence of any systematic force determining the outcome of any one roll and supported by the failure of any known "system" to predict accurately such random events. The sophisticated gambler need only argue that his system transcends such naive arguments in order to convince himself that the statisticians' propositions about randomness do not apply to his case.

A final difficulty is the fact that many modern scientific theories are not really theories at all, but only conclusions derived from the weight of the evidence. The American Cancer Society has not proven that cigarettes cause cancer, but only that there seems to exist a substantial statistical relationship between smoking and respiratory illnesses. The failure to specify a causal mechanism opens the possibility that the scientific theories themselves are incorrect: just as the gambler believes that metaphysical influences govern the spin of roulette wheels, the tobacco companies might argue that respiratory illness is associated with personality characteristics which also just happen to be causally associated with cigarette smoking. It is indeed possible that it is we, ourselves, who are caught in the ignorance trap and not the so-called victims. We may be so entranced by the thought that we know better than these victims that *we* are the ones who subscribe to entirely false views of the world.

It is not much help that scientists themselves are an intolerant lot. One does not induce a trap victim to abandon a false theory by stressing his stupidity or the absurdity of the theory itself, and yet members of the teaching profession appear occasionally to derive so much satisfaction from accusing others of ignorance, guilt, or outright malevolence that they take themselves into an arena in which conflict dominates knowledge and the trap remains unresolved. If our objective is to encourage a new viewpoint to displace an entrapping theory, we must proceed by reinforcing the right model, rather than punishing the wrong one.

Adding Punishment to the Bait

If gambling is immoral, then at least those who wish to avoid social opprobrium will stay out of the trap, and to that extent the development of social standards of moral conduct may be effective in punishing those who take the bait. Objections to this use of social pressure are often based upon the assertion that gambling is simply another example of a victimless crime which can harm only the gambler—a view which reflects the usual reliance upon rationality as a model of behavior. A more cogent objection might be that once we have branded gambling as immoral, we have rescued only those individuals who are actually influenced by concern for their own standards of conduct; at the same time, we have precluded the development of various alternative remedies (such as the government's providing a "fair" lottery) because they would appear to be unethical, as well.

When we label certain behaviors "immoral," we render socially unacceptable those remedies that involve regulating, rather than forbidding, the behavior, because the remedies are now tainted by the same immorality as the taboo behavior itself. The only remaining remedies may themselves create a host of attendant problems. American attempts to deal with heroin, cocaine, and marijuana consumption are often cited as examples of this. In the United States the consumption of drugs is strictly forbidden and the government is committed to the eradication of supplies and the jailing of dealers and traffickers. A consequence of this policy of prohibition is that the price of illicit drugs rises to the point at which it is commensu-

rate with the risk that government policy has imposed on dealers. (Indeed, enforcement agencies often gauge their effectiveness in blocking supplies by looking at the street price of
drugs.) Unquestionably, these high prices will deter some
users, particularly those entering the trap for the first time,
because they successfully add a new punishment to the bait.
On the other hand, those who are still in the trap must find
adequate financial resources to support their expensive habits,
and they often do so by committing various crimes of theft or
by becoming dealers themselves. Our streets have become un-
safe and our homes vulnerable to burglary largely because
drug users require so much more economic support. Thus,
while American policy may have achieved some success in
inhibiting addiction, it has at the same time imposed a cost of
its own by shifting a large part of the burden of the addicts'
trap onto the public at large. Opponents of this policy argue
that the number of potential addicts saved does not justify this
enormous new social cost, and that we have therefore moved
into a worse trap than the one which we had before.

The British experience provides an interesting contrast. In
Britain, the government becomes "the Man" and, within limits, provides addicts with an inexpensive, noncriminal source
of drugs. Under this system, addicts need not resort to criminal activities to pay for their habits; moreover, the development of an underworld marketplace and its attendant problems is inhibited. It is easier to be an addict in Britain, but the
streets are safer.

Social pressures are often used to punish entry into superstition traps. Ridicule is a very effective reinforcer in inducing
behavior change, and behavior which is inconsistent with accepted logical rules is certain to be scoffed at sooner or later.
Unfortunately, ridicule also provides a powerful inducement
for the victim to justify his behavior, giving added impetus to
the development of theories which can then generalize a trap
far beyond its original boundaries. Our baseball pitcher in-
vents his theory of muscle tone so that sports announcers will
not take every opportunity to describe his idiosyncrasies to

their audiences. Similarly, once the primitive farmer has acquired the routine of planting a fish next to his seeds, the temptation to invent a god that requires this sacrifice is very strong. The tendency to invent theories to justify behavior patterns which are superstitiously acquired only compounds the problems. The baseball pitcher is in a trap, but it is a trivial one unless the theory devised as a defense against social ridicule leads him to engage in further exercises that are harmful. The farmer is not in a trap at all, since the fish fertilizes his soil, but his theology may create a god who eventually requires far more substantial sacrifices.

In summary, our commitment to rationality as the only acceptable basis for behavior often leads us to punish those we perceive to be in ignorance traps. If, because of our generally limited supply of scientific knowledge, we are wrong, or if our victim is forced to concoct a plausible justification for his behavior, we have compounded a trap rather than prevented one.

Trap Insurance

Even if we do not prevent ignorance traps, we can protect their victims against devastating loss by spreading the cost over the society. The stock market speculator who suffers disastrous losses is at least protected by our bankruptcy laws from eternal indebtedness. The speeding teenager who survives his automobile crash because of federally mandated safety equipment in his car has benefited at the expense of everybody who has paid the higher prices on automobiles. It would be equally possible, if we wished, to provide special federal welfare benefits for those who have suffered from gambling losses.

As in the case of time-delay traps, there is the problem that trap insurance would influence the incidence of ignorance traps: bankruptcy laws make speculation less risky and safe automobile design reduces the dangers from speeding. Usually, the behavioral influence of insurance would be attenuated by the same factors that created the traps in the first place. If the teenager is undeterred by the danger of a crash, he may be equally unaffected by a lessening of the danger. The teenager who was not trapped because he feared a crash may now enter, however, because the fear is somewhat relieved. Of course, in the case of gambling, insurance has a substantive effect on the situation. As we have already observed, "fair" insurance (i.e., insurance paid for by gamblers themselves) would eliminate the trap. Subsidized insurance (paid for by everyone) would change the odds, and anyone who qualified for its benefits would find that further losses would be partially, or even wholly, reimbursed; consequently, the only existing disincentive for gambling would vanish. In this case, then, trap insurance could only worsen the problem.

Superordinate Authority

Since ignorance traps have the general property of generating theories that justify the behavior, making voluntary escapes less likely, the temptation is very great to resort to some superordinate authority to resolve the problem. In some cases, this amounts simply to making the trap illegal; one may ban gambling or restrict short-term trading on the stock market in order to remove these random elements from people's lives. In other cases, one may seek a remedy through technocracy. For example, if the basis of a trap lies in a general acceptance of a fallacious theory, then, in principle at least, an escape lies in transferring decision-making authority to the "experts"— those individuals who through specialization and study have become more familiar than the rest of society with the processes involved. That is, we could give economists and businessmen sole responsibility for managing the economy, sociologists and psychologists would have responsibility for our prison and rehabilitation systems, and political scientists together with State Department experts would handle all foreign policy. Naturally this presumes that the experts are wholly objective in their appraisal of circumstances; and certainly, before we put so much power into the hands of the scientists and engineers, we ought to assure ourselves that they are genuinely enlightened, and not merely subject to ignorance traps different from those which afflict the rest of society. Technocracy stands as a solution only so long as we have confidence in the reliability of the experts, for their knowledge—because of its highly technical nature—is not of a sort readily communicable to the general public.

5

Sliding Reinforcers

Four Horsemen of the Apocalypse

Albrecht Dürer
woodcut 1498

Described in the book of Revelation (6:2–8) as possessing "power over the fourth part of the earth, to kill with the sword and with hunger," the horsemen dramatize a fifteenth-century view of the human capacity to bring war and pestilence upon mankind.

A farmer sprays his fields with DDT in order to eliminate insects which attack his crops. The immediate consequence is the encouraging absence of pests a few hours later. This in turn leads to a subsequent reward in the form of increased crop yield. The following year, however, the insects return. Experience being the great teacher, the problem appears to have an easy solution: the DDT is applied again, and again the insects die. This cycle may be repeated over several years, and the DDT becomes recognized as an effective agent for dealing with the insect problem. Eventually, however, a time comes when the DDT loses some of its effectiveness: the infestation of insects is reduced, but not entirely eliminated. Reasoning that if some is good, more is better, the farmer soon discovers that the loss of effectiveness may be remedied through an increase in the dosage, and the cycle continues as before with the elaboration that, whenever the insecticide appears diminished in effectiveness, the dosage is increased to levels adequate to do the job. At last, as we now know, a day arrives when the DDT is sprayed but the insects seem unaffected by their chemical diet. How is the farmer to respond? A further increase in dosage sufficient to eliminate the pests may both be too expensive and so thoroughly poison the crop that it is better sold as insecticide than as food. At the same time, the insects' natural enemies—birds and reptiles—seem to have disappeared, so that abandonment of the pesticide program now would make the farmer worse off than he would have been had the program never been initiated. The trap has been sprung, with the farmer neatly caught inside.

At first glance this may seem to be a version of a time-delay trap, but, though there are time-delay features, the essential element in the example is the fact that the behavior in question is *initially entirely reasonable*. The first dose of DDT is large enough to eliminate the insects and small enough not to harm other wildlife. If the farmer were to refrain from reapplications of the pesticide, he would gain one exceptionally good crop year and suffer no long-term losses. It is the repeated use of the insecticide that leads to the trap, for due to the persistence of DDT, each application actually changes the payoff structure facing the farmer on future occasions, and eventually this payoff structure becomes dominated by punishment. In addition, the effectiveness of the DDT is progressively diminished because natural selection of the insect population results in the emergence of a strain of pesticide-resistant insects. We have an instance here of a behavior whose reward diminishes with repeated occurrences of the behavior. If the reward level is to be maintained at a fixed level, the behavior must be more "vigorous," and greater amounts of effort must be exerted in order to produce the rewarding consequences.

In the sliding-reinforcer situation, the behavior may also be followed by a punishment that can be alleviated by a repetition of the initial behavior. In our example, the use of DDT depleted the insects' natural predators, and this in turn led to larger infestations than would have occurred naturally. Further applications of DDT then became the only means to alleviate this punishment. Just as repeated occurrences of the behavior produce diminishing magnitudes of reward, so these punishments may require a repeat of the behavior at greater levels of intensity for effective alleviation. Eventually the time may come when the cost of avoiding the punishment exceeds the rewards which the behavior had succeeded in producing at any time, but by now the individual is locked in, and abandonment of the behavior can lead only to disaster.

Since they both occur across time, there is some similarity between sliding-reinforcer and time-delay traps. The time-delay trap, like the sliding-reinforcer trap, is baited with an immediate reward that follows the particular behavior. However, in the time-delay situation the behavior only needs to occur once. The trap arises because the immediate reward is followed by a delayed punishment of greater magnitude than the reward. The delay in the punishment causes its magnitude to be underestimated, and this leads the victim to pay for a small gain with a large loss. In the sliding-reinforcer situation it is temporal repetition which leads to the trap: behavior in the present leads to punishment in the future because it in-duces the same trapped behavior to recur in the future. Time-delay traps are usually much simpler than sliding-reinforcer traps because they do not include any temptation for their victims to repeat the behavior simply to relieve the punishment brought on by the behavior itself. Eating does not offset the punishments which follow gluttony, increased cigarette smoking does not produce even temporary relief of cancer symptoms, and making new credit purchases certainly does not eliminate one's debts. In contrast, repeated sprayings of DDT *do* produce a temporary elimination of insects and an injection of heroin *will* temporarily relieve the symptoms of withdrawal. In these examples of sliding reinforcers, behavior that appears to offer some reward in fact exacerbates the problem it was intended to solve in a way which also encourages a repeat of the behavior, leading the individual into a cycle where things go from bad to worse in spite of increasing efforts by the individual to improve things.

Sliding-reinforcer traps arise because behavior which is repeatedly rewarded becomes habitual, and the habit thus acquired carries over into more ambiguous circumstances. If behavior were entirely rational, the punishments could be avoided because the behavior would cease as soon as it became inappropriate. The rational farmer would abandon DDT as soon as its damage to wildlife and increasing insect resistance began to offset its contribution to larger crops. The mechanism of learning, unfortunately, is not so accommodating; it is one's past successes that largely determine one's present behavior, and even an intellectual awareness that conditions have changed is not sufficient to change well-established habits.

We include in the category of sliding-reinforcer traps situations that incorporate this habit-formation dimension alone, as well as those which involve a direct dynamic link between sequences of behavior and sequence of reward. Cases which do not include dynamic links are those in which the reward structure changes but a learned pattern of behavior persists, at least for a while. Examples of such "simple" sliding-reinforcer traps are very common. Thus, if you should happen to wear your shoes in a mosque or eat off your knife at a dinner party, you may be acting in ways that are entirely conventional and reasonable for the circumstances in which you typically find yourself; despite awareness that your behavior should be adapted to suit these new conditions, the habits which have been formed under ordinary reinforcing situations stubbornly persist and may even lead to punishment. The man who is regularly rewarded for telling obscene stories at work, at lunch, at his club, or at office Christmas parties may find it hard to build enough discrimination into his habits to avoid repetitions of these performances at meetings of his church vestry or at dinner parties at home. In these simple traps, the reward structures that confront individuals are sometimes changed because the general environment has changed; as a result, many individuals are trapped in parallel, producing an aggregation of punishments that affect the entire society. For instance, during the nineteenth century, the relatively high death rate among children—together with the abundance of resources in this country—meant that raising large families was sensible and productive. Over the years, large families came to acquire large positive values in our culture. Today, child mortality rates are much lower and there no longer seems to be a need for more labor in our economy. Nevertheless, we find the old behavior persisting: decades after it has ceased to be appropriate, audiences in television studios still applaud enthusiastically when a housewife with ten children is introduced, and large families are frequently described and eulogized in the women's pages of our larger newspapers. Only very recently has the value of a large family begun to be questioned, occurring many years after most observers had concluded that it was no longer functional.

Social institutions are the public counterparts of personal habits and can produce simple sliding-reinforcer traps in the same way as individuals. Patterns of behavior that are appropriate at one point in time can be institutionalized and continue to win formal support long after their social value has passed. This, we suppose, was a major factor in maintaining a high birth rate in the United States for so long. Even now we retain a variety of institutionalized incentives that encourage parents to raise larger families. Prevention of childbirth has been difficult: dissemination of birth control information was, until recently, illegal; most abortions were, until recently, illegal; many religious institutions are still vehemently opposed to any but the most ineffective attempts at birth control. Moreover, we have institutional devices that reduce the individual family cost of child raising by spreading the economic burden throughout the rest of society. Income taxes are reduced in proportion to the number of children in the family, medical insurance does not depend upon family size, public schooling spreads the major expense of children—education—across all the residents of a geographic area, and the present call for free, publicly supported day-care centers is essentially a demand for further reduction in the personal cost of bearing children. Inevitably a decrease in the cost of offspring leads to an increase in their number, thereby interfering with any policy of population control. We recognize that many of these programs were motivated by concerns other than support for large families; nevertheless, it is surely true that were large numbers of children regarded as "bad," rather than "good" as they have been traditionally, alternative means would have been developed for addressing these concerns which did not at the same time exacerbate a trap.

In the last chapter, we discussed some mechanisms by which theories could be reinforced and noted that the generalization of certain theories could lead to ignorance traps. The same observations apply to sliding-reinforcer traps. Examples that most often arise in this regard involve the development of rules and procedures for solving problems. If one type of approach to problems of a given class is found to pay off repeatedly, that same type of approach will be utilized again whenever another problem in that class arises and, so long as it is successful, this habitual application will be reinforced. Devotees of mathematical or geometric puzzles will recognize this fact as the underlying principle of the brainteaser. The best kind of puzzle is one whose presentation triggers the use of a particular set of habitual solution techniques but where these are just the techniques that will *not* work. "On a piece of paper, place a square array of nine dots, three dots on a side, and then connect all nine dots by drawing a connected sequence of four straight lines such that each dot lies upon at least one line." The structure of this problem is quite straightforward, yet many people experience difficulty in discovering a satisfactory solution. The difficulty is not inherent in the puzzle, but arises from our habitual procedure of connecting dots with lines that begin with one dot and end with another and from our inclination to limit the extent of our drawing to the confines of the square box defined by the array. In order to solve the problem, one must break both of these habits.

Though different in other respects, sliding-reinforcer traps share with time-delay traps an important dynamic dimension. The pattern according to which reinforcements change over time will determine the strength of the habit, the strength of the resulting punishments, and even one's ability to recognize the trap itself. A dramatic or abrupt shift in reinforcement schedules can make a great contribution toward rational behavior by providing an unmistakable signal of a change in circumstances. As an illustration, consider the sort of situation faced by a career civil servant who works directly below a political appointee. Suppose that after an election his superior is replaced by someone who is loyal to another party. Habits of speech and attitude that were most strongly reinforced before are anathema to the successor, and if they have become habitual, the civil servant can expect difficulties in obtaining future rewards. A potentially saving feature of this trap is the abruptness of the change in the sort of behavior that will be rewarded, because this provides an obvious indicator that the situation has turned into a trap. Even if the civil servant had taken full advantage of the rewards available during the tenancy of his first superior, the distinctness of the change in circumstances will alert him to the importance of modifying his behavior, enabling him to take steps to break his habitual mode of behavior. He may even succeed in developing a new pattern that is particularly gratifying to his new boss, thereby receiving even higher returns.

The subtlety and effectiveness of a sliding-reinforcer trap is greatly increased if the transition is gradual. Suppose that the entrapping behavior initially produces greater benefits than its alternatives and that the deterioration in its rewards is so moderate that the victim may have slid into the range of punishment long before realizing that anything is wrong. Since there is no sharp line dividing the rewarding circumstances from the punishing ones, entrapment is very likely. The gradual process of aging provides many examples of traps which follow this dynamic pattern. Typically, a child may be rewarded for various childish behavior patterns: imperfections in speech, outspokenness, occasional tears, strongly self-centered behavior, exhibitionism, the "playful" acting out of even violent conflict, and sometimes cruelty to animals and playmates. At the same time, many potentially unpleasant behavior patterns go unpunished: a messy room, noisemaking, personal insults directed at friends and acquaintances, ungenerous interpersonal relationships, and so forth. Much of the behavior that is permitted or found endearing in children is not tolerated in adults, however, and as an accompaniment to growing up, the rewards attached to such behaviors will disappear and be replaced by punishments. The child who does not adapt in a timely way to these changed circumstances is in a sliding-reinforcer trap. The adolescent, particularly, is in such a trap, having to unlearn much of what had been previously rewarded and having to learn to do things which previously had never been rewarded. Moreover, the process of adapting our behavior does not by any means stop at adolescence. The single male with a good job may develop patterns of consumption that prove entirely inappropriate after marriage, the married couple may develop behavior and consumption patterns which are quite unsuitable after the arrival of children, the proud parent may develop attitudes and relationships toward children that are entirely inappropriate after the children have reached maturity, and, finally, the physical exertion that is normal or even stimulating during one's youth becomes difficult and possibly even fatal. With every major snowstorm in our northern cities there are reports of citizens who, although they had shoveled their sidewalks and driveways all their lives, had reached an age at which such exertion was no longer possible and had triggered heart attacks. By applying behavioral rules which had been established years before, these individuals became victims.

Excessive population growth can also be interpreted as the type of trap characterized by gradual (almost imperceptible) deterioration in rewards. Worse, the gradual growth in population is itself the source of further traps. Knowing what the birth rate has been over the last twenty years, we can predict with virtual certainty that the need for living space and for agricultural produce will continue to expand. It has been the case ever since North America was settled, however, that land was abundantly available, and there has been no need to develop living or agricultural patterns to conserve it. Consequently, we have developed residential and transportation habits that heavily use the land. Our cities, instead of maintaining high population concentrations, are decentralizing into scattered suburbs that encroach upon agricultural land, along with requiring further space for road and parking facilities. Furthermore, this habit of urban decentralization has been institutionalized into government subsidy programs that support residential construction and road building, making the suburban life-style possible. The changed circumstances in terms of growing scarcity of formerly abundant resources have not yet been dramatic enough, however, to make it clear that these programs are no longer appropriate, and we are likely now to be sliding into a predictable trap.

The farmer who sprays excessive DDT on his crops and the drug user who traps himself into addiction are also victims of situations that are characterized by gradual changes in reward patterns, but unlike simple traps, they are complicated by the fact that the reduction in reward is a consequence of behavior itself. DDT would never lose its effectiveness if it were never used, or only used very sparingly, and drug addiction comes about only as a consequence of use. An example of this same property is found in popular mythology: the boy who cried "wolf" found himself in a trap because it was his own unwarranted cries for help that brought him the gratification of receiving attention but which, at the same time, cost him his credibility. These "endogenous" deteriorations in reward magnitudes may be more insidious than those found in simple traps because they provide no external signal of a change in circumstances. Our man who tells an obscene story at a vestry meeting does know where he is, and the person in an age-related sliding-reinforcer trap at least suspects a connection between age and sensible behavior. In these instances there are external indicators of one's position vis-à-vis available rewards and punishments, and persons with sufficient self-control have an opportunity to adjust their behavior and adapt to changes in circumstances. The endogenous traps, however, provide no such signals: the child who sings "Row, Row, Row, Your Boat" fifteen times before eliciting punishment from an exasperated parent may receive many warnings before being punished, but unless the parent is remarkably consistent, regularly carrying out every threat, the child has no way of knowing just when the shift from reward to punishment will actually come about.

When combined with an element of time delay, sliding-reinforcer traps take on a special capacity for locking in their victims. Returning to the situation of the DDT-spraying farmer: repeated applications of the insecticide reduce its immediate effectiveness and at the same time add future punishments to the act of stopping, because the associated destruction of the insects' natural enemies increases future crop damage. If the farmer is not sufficiently farsighted to take account of future losses attributable to the DDT, then the only relevant reinforcers are those which operate in the present, and the use of DDT will always be preferred to nonuse. Indeed, DDT has consistently positive benefits until a point is reached at which the crop itself is unfit for human consumption. The determination of rational behavior against which we can compare the farmer's trap is not simply a matter of taking account of future punishments that are contingent upon the use of DDT. Those punishments are influenced by how much insecticide is used later on, as well. The rational farmer must develop a program of annual DDT use not only by comparing the short-run benefits of insect destruction against the long-run damage suffered as a consequence of the elimination of the insects' predators, but also by deciding whether an acceptable further dose of the poison is more profitably applied now or sometime in the future. In principle, the means for performing this analysis are available. Although they are difficult, the mathematical tools necessary to do the calculations are well known to specialists in operations research and to economists; they can be applied as soon as the farmer has established an appropriate weighting of present benefits against future losses and has determined the technical relationship between this year's use of DDT and the benefits and costs of future use.

It is the thesis of this book, however, that our "rational" farmer is an outrageously overoptimistic invention. Even if we were to accept the proposition that the farmer had access to the technical knowledge and the mathematical ability necessary to follow the optimal program dictated by rationality, psychological principles of behavior do not support a contention that this is the course we could expect the farmer to follow. It is certain that if he follows the usual guides to behavior, permitting himself to be influenced principally by immediate benefits, the apparent rewards of DDT use will be much too high. The farmer who overlooks the time-delay element in the trap may not even question the value of insecticide until he reaches the point where its insect-killing potential is negligible. This is a point far beyond that at which the rational farmer would have found that the loss attributable to DDT use began to exceed the benefit. To the rational farmer, limits to DDT use are part of the same program under which the applications of the insecticide were initiated. For the trapped farmer, however, termination of the DDT program represents an entirely different behavior, having its own rewards, and once he is in a trap, his prior use of DDT influences the present and future consequences of discontinuance as well as the consequences of the use itself. The insidiousness of the trap rests in the fact that there is no point at which immediate payoffs to these behaviors are reversed: the short-run payoffs for DDT *always* exceed the payoffs for nonuse. Suppose, for example, that DDT has been used up to a point at which the farmer's rewards are even less than before DDT was invented, so that the farmer is worse off than he would have been had it never been used. There is still no reward for stopping: if the farmer refrains from subsequent use of the poison, the disappearance of the insects' natural predators means that the payoff is even further reduced. Weighing choices only in terms of current rewards, it is always better to continue to use the poison than to stop. Even when both behaviors lead to actual punishment, the relationship holds, and the victim is inexorably driven deeper and deeper into the trap.

We may view the drug-addiction problem along similar lines. Initial doses of most addictive drugs are not dangerously debilitating, and if for one reason or another such limited consumption is rewarded, a rational pattern of behavior may be compatible with some indulgence. Indeed, it is this fact that is so often used to justify early experimentation with drugs. Experimental levels of drug consumption, however, may be sufficient to make abstention mildly punishing, and whereas the "rational" plan includes limits on drug consumption in the face of these punishments, anyone whose behavior is guided by the more immediate pressures of short-run reinforcers will be driven to further use. In terms of current rewards and punishments, continued drug use still is preferred to nonuse, and the individual will never reach a point at which the learning mechanism will bring this destructive indulgence to an end.

In addressing such problems as drug addiction, it is important to recognize that the entrapment does not come from the drug alone, but from the drug in combination with the mechanism of reinforcement learning. Too often one hears of parents or educators attempting to combat drug experimentation with assertions that the drugs, themselves, are poisonous. Such people are appealing to a rational model of behavior for their arguments: rational people do not take poison, therefore as soon as one "knows" that drugs are poison, one will avoid them. Such arguments are self-defeating on two points. Once a child or teenager sees someone else use a drug with no apparent ill effects, the image of drug-as-poison is destroyed, at least for short-run use. Then the implicit appeal to rational behavior actually *encourages* use, because one can describe a rational behavioral program which includes limited drug consumption. The real culprit in the drug-addiction trap is the mistaken belief that our behavior is guided solely by rational principles, and that we can follow optimal behavioral programs whatever the pattern of rewards and punishments over time may be. The phrase "I can stop whenever I want to" is not merely a symptom, but constitutes the trap itself.

There is no paradox in the conclusion that rational behavior might require that an individual pursue a course of action up to a point at which stopping produces immediate punishing consequences. Continuing so far may well be justified when the unpleasantness associated with terminating the behavior is more than offset by earlier gains (such as the farmer's increased crop yields). On the other hand, it is clear that this policy makes immense demands on one's self-control. By the time we arrive at the stopping point, stopping has become painful and further indulgence is a ready means for avoiding that pain. Belief in rationality is what got us into this predicament. Many social conventions have been devised to assist us in avoiding these traps ("never use drugs," "ban DDT," "drink only at mealtime"), but these conventions are easily disrupted by a belief in rationality and the recognition that small indulgences never did anyone any harm. If behavior is not governed by such simple logic, however, and if the individual, while correct in evaluating the objective situation, is nonetheless incorrect in appreciating the forces determining his own behavior, indulgence will begin and the trap will close.

Ways Out

Sliding-reinforcer traps arise when sensible behavior is carried too far or is repeated too often. The trap is not the qualitative one of choosing an entirely inappropriate action; it is the quantitative one of overindulgence. Had the boy who cried "wolf" confined his prank to only one occasion, he would have been able to enjoy his joke without suffering the loss of assistance when the real emergency arose. The farmer could use DDT sparingly without appreciably reducing the population of useful insect predators; even a drug user can justify his initial consumption by showing that no damage results.

Those trap avoidance techniques which depend upon bait avoidance may not be successful when the entrapping situation is one that produces large benefits before the gains begin to be transformed into losses. Even today a controversy rages over the use of DDT to control malaria-carrying mosquitoes in many developing countries. Despite the well-publicized detrimental side effects of heavy use of DDT, governments in these nations feel that the contemporary reduction in human death and suffering justifies its use, and they often interpret attempts to halt the use of DDT as an attack upon their national aspirations. The validity of this position is hard to appraise. Whether or not the circumstances constitute a trap depends on the values that these nations place upon the natural resources damaged by insecticides. The example does point up, however, how tricky are the pitfalls in any attempt to judge whether someone else is in a trap. Necessarily, a trap is defined in terms of one's own values. Accordingly, anyone who has outside interests and who claims that punishments "ought" to be weighed more heavily or more lightly cannot be given much standing. In the final analysis, the only one who can identify any trap with authority is the victim himself.

As with time-delay and ignorance traps, remedies for sliding-reinforcer traps may be affected by making the underlying trade-offs more explicit, by modifying the existing reinforcement schedules (such as giving methadone in order to block the rewarding power of heroin), or by associating punishments with the bait (some behavior-modification therapists treat alcoholism by pairing an electric shock with drinking in the clinic). The principles underlying these remedies and examples of most of them have been discussed in the last two chapters. We will not repeat the discussion here. The unique feature of sliding-reinforcer traps is that initially successful behavior continues and carries over into situations for which it is no longer appropriate, and it is this persistence which the ideal remedy would control. If we can extinguish a habit before it begins to generate punishments, then we will have enjoyed the earlier rewards without paying the price that goes with having fallen into the trap. Many psychologists feel that punishment is a means for accomplishing the extinction of a learned behavior, and in this vein we find some parents punishing their offspring for childish behavior before social situations are encountered in which the behavior would be seriously inappropriate. Similarly, doctors urge their elderly patients not to overly exert themselves (e.g., by shoveling snow) in hopes of forestalling serious illness.

Though punishment may be effective, the best means for extinguishing one habit is to develop and reward behavior that is incompatible with it. If our farmer were converted into a devoted bird-watcher, his overuse of DDT would be less likely to occur because there would be new rewards for non-use. Drug addiction and alcoholism come about when one has no predominating need for a state of mental alertness, and when one feels a need for social approval from acquaintances who already use drugs, rather than from those who do not. In the last analysis, we cannot combat the drug trap by convincing those who succumb to it that drugs are bad, but we can demonstrate that some competing alternatives are better.

Unless the punishment is long delayed or is so cataclysmic

as to forestall further learning, most habits will be successfully extinguished after they begin to encounter punishments; at most, therefore, simple sliding-reinforcer traps are only temporarily painful. When a time-delay element is introduced, however, the direction taken by the learning mechanism is reversed: the farmer and the drug user are driven into the trap, instead of out of it. In these cases remedies must be sought either through the use of conventional means to prevent the behavior altogether (ban DDT or make drug consumption illegal) or, if we believe the initial benefits of the behavior to be so large as to justify the risk, we must find some means to reverse ourselves when the time comes, moving directly contrary to the pressures of the established reinforcement schedule. The simplest means for doing this would be to commit ourselves in advance to some new punishment whose administration is contingent upon the behavior occurring beyond its optimal stopping point. The teenager who justifies his experimentation with drugs with the assertion that he can stop at some specified level can, with equal confidence, enter into a binding contract to mow every lawn in suburban Westchester County should that point be exceeded. The heavy drinker who is sure that he can control his consumption should be willing to guarantee to contribute half his income to his state's mental health program if a specified limit to his alcohol consumption is ever exceeded. The farmer who plans to limit his use of DDT anyway should willingly agree to contribute his profits to the Sierra Club should that limit be passed.

The point is that the real danger in time-delay sliding-reinforcer traps lies in overconfidence. It is in the belief that objective rationality can be made to govern our behavior despite the directives of reinforcement learning that we initiate potentially harmful behavior without, at the same time, taking steps to ensure that we will stop before the harm arrives. Once this danger is recognized, these traps can be avoided. If we begin a behavior by planning to halt at some point, then we should have no hesitation in committing ourselves to even very large punishments if we should fail to stop at that point. No harm is done—since we plan to stop there anyway, there is nothing to fear from the contract. To the one who believes that rationality is the foundation of behavior, such a commitment is innocuous and there can be no objections to it. To the believer in reinforcement learning, such a commitment is essential and provides the only protection one has against a dangerous trap.

6 *Who Got My Reinforcer?*

Le Mauvais Côté des Nouveaux Omnibus

Honoré Daumier lithograph 1856

The new (double-decker) buses have an unfortunate property in that one passenger, in pursuing his own ends, may incidentally tread on the well-being of another.

Professor Thomas Schelling of Harvard University has described a neat little example of a trap. On a Sunday evening in summer, thousands of Bostonians are working their ways home from Cape Cod on narrow, twisting, two-lane roads. A mattress which has fallen off a station wagon has been left abandoned in the center of the homebound lane, and a traffic jam has developed for some distance behind it. Nevertheless, no one moves the mattress. When each automobile reaches the head of the line, the driver simply waits for a break in the traffic in the opposite lane, skirts around the mattress, and continues on. Though it would be easy for someone at the head of the jam to stop, get out, and move the mattress out of everyone's way, it is nevertheless faster, once one has reached that point, to stay in the car, wait for the break in the oncoming traffic, and go ahead. While anyone who has reached the mattress has the power to take action that would benefit those behind, it would be at some personal cost in the form of work effort and additional delay in getting home. It is a property of the situation, moreover, that everyone in the line will sooner or later get to the mattress, and thus everyone has a turn at being the driver whose inaction is responsible for the suffering of those who will come later. Farther back in the line, each may curse the lack of public spiritedness responsible for the delay, but upon reaching the mattress, the circumstances change. It is quicker to get home by staying in the car, and so each proceeds on his way, now the object of his own condemnation. Such traps can occur whenever the activities that one individual pursues produce consequences for both himself and others, and when the rewards and punishments which shape the behavior of one individual do not match the payoffs which that behavior brings to others. The barbecue gourmet enjoys his charcoaled delicacies, but his downwind neighbors get only the smoke.

We have called such traps "externality" traps in order to follow the terminology widely used by economists. The mattress-induced traffic jam is an example of the kind of externality trap often produced by queues. Queues are especially likely to turn into traps because of the unavoidable control over the welfare of others that is exerted by whomever is at the front of the line. The driver of a slow-moving truck who does not let anyone pass, the customer at the cash register in a cafeteria line who wishes to pay by check, and the client in line at the bank who does not complete his paperwork until actually arriving at the teller's window all provide examples in which one person, by avoiding small inconvenience to himself, imposes inconvenience upon everyone behind. Because of the large number of persons who can be affected, a small personal benefit to the person in front can be multiplied into quite a large collective loss.

It is no solution to assert that these traps arise only because some people are rude or lack public spirit. The problem is simply that the rewards guiding people's behavior are leading in the wrong directions. Certainly, increases in social consciousness would be beneficial; a public-spirited truck driver would pull over for a few minutes to let people pass, and a more responsible bank client would sign his checks beforehand, but human nature being what it is, even our perceptions of which behavior is proper and public-spirited is likely to be influenced by the circumstances. The truck driver may see himself as engaging in a productive endeavor in which his time has a real economic value, whereas those behind him are merely vacationers on their way to the beach. The customer cashing a check in a cafeteria attributes the delay to the cashier's unnecessary insistence on personal identification and a silly demand for the manager's approval, rather than to his own behavior. To be effective, a code of queuing ethics would probably have to be quite specific ("one does not cash checks in cafeterias" or "truck drivers shall pull over when they retard traffic"), rather than relying upon generalities that are open to individual interpretations.

As traps, these queuing examples are intriguing, but individually they rarely amount to more than minor irritations. Nevertheless, the principle they demonstrate extends very far: individual behavior is not governed so much by who one is or

what one "thinks," as it is by where one is and what reinforcers operate on one's present position. This fact is familiar
to students of political processes. American political history
abounds with examples of men whose political orientation appeared to undergo dramatic change after succession to some
relatively invulnerable political office. Some of our most liberal
supreme court justices have been selected because of their
conservative credentials; and some of our most conservative
justices were installed by ostensibly liberal administrations. It
is, of course, possible that these men were masquerading
throughout their political careers, only letting their true colors
show after achievement of a life tenancy on the court. More
likely, however, these men simply found themselves confronted by radically new sets of reinforcers at the same time
that many old reinforcers associated with elections and temporary appointments fell away. Gradually habits changed, opinions changed, and even overall political outlooks shifted from
one pole to the other. In the same vein, we noted at the beginning of this book that it is a mistake to believe that the operations of some governmental department would be drastically
altered by placing new individuals in leadership positions.
The new leaders would find themselves subject to the same
conditions and the same reinforcers as did their predecessors.
Insofar as the new leaders represent a different political party,
their behavior may be modified to be responsive to the reinforcers associated with a different political tradition; nevertheless, in the complex of contingencies which surrounds them,
these political reinforcers would represent only a small part of
the entire spectrum of consequences that affect behavior.

The problem of externality traps is by no means new to the
social sciences. For many years, economists have been familiar
with the problems created by individual acts of consumption
or production which impose unintended losses upon others,
and these interactions comprise one of the major classes of
impediments to the effective functioning of a market system.
Usually, two subclasses are distinguished: *externalities in consumption* describe cases in which one person's consumption

(or nonconsumption) affects the welfare of someone else; *externalities in production* describe those cases in which the manufacture or distribution of some useful commodity generates an incidental byproduct that is of little interest to the manufacturer but which has great influence over the welfare of other members of society. Although production externalities come most frequently to mind (particularly in the form of industrial pollution), the consumption externality appears to be more fundamental in principle, and it is therefore this second class to which we turn first.

Consumption Externalities

Many consumption externalities result merely from differences in personal taste. Suppose that Peter, an office worker, were to arrive in the morning wearing a sports jacket of a particularly nauseous shade of yellow, a green polka-dot tie, orange slacks, and white shoes. His horrified fellow employees may find that this style of dress not only offends their eyes but is so distracting as to interfere with their work. However intangible this aesthetic conflict may seem to be, Peter has imposed a loss on his fellows which interferes with their comfort and well-being in as substantial a way as does the truck driver whose slow progress holds up a long line of cars or the vacationer who fails to move a mattress out of the road. One may be tempted to believe that someone who offends our sensibilities is doing insubstantial harm compared to someone who wastes our time, but this reaction is surely predicated on an overvaluation of time and inadequate concern for environment. There is also the difficulty of measurement of "loss" when an aesthetic assault occurs. The essentially subjective nature of aesthetic interests makes difficult an evaluation of losses. Our courts are reluctant even to hear cases in which a party seeks to recover damages in compensation for an aesthetic trespass or nuisance. The difficulty of associating any tangible value to a subjective loss makes this an area of interpersonal conflict in which few legal remedies are available.

The opportunities for consumption externalities are bound-less, and each of us encounters them daily. Our friend Peter may have just moved into a conservative residential area and painted his house in purple and gold stripes. He plays his stereo system loudly until two o'clock in the morning. He owns four cars, all customized with racing slicks and painted with dragons and fire, two of which must be parked on the street for lack of garage space. He has a sunflower garden for a front lawn, and he regularly attends the neighborhood church dressed in a more flamboyant version of his everyday style. In spite of his flashy cars, he drives slowly on high-ways and is very cautious in making left turns at stop lights with the result that those behind him usually have to wait for the light to turn green on the next time around (another queuing example). Not to be left out, his wife wears hair curlers to the supermarket and habitually leaves her shopping cart in the middle of the aisle while foraging for groceries. The list could go on and on. The unhappiness caused by this kind of behavior is substantial, especially if many instances cumulate during the course of one day, but normally none of this unhappiness is intended (our example thus does not in-clude those who deliberately wear dirty clothes and stringy hair if their object is, in part, to offend someone else). No doubt each of us engages in one or more of these behaviors at some time or other, not because we wish to antagonize or offend others, but simply because they accompany behavior which is rewarding for ourselves.

Obviously these consumption externalities lead to traps, al-though we generally do not worry about many of them be-cause they arise from symmetric antagonisms between indi-vidual preferences. The neighbors around the purple- and gold-painted house may very well assert that they know who is responsible for the trouble, but in doing so, they are only reflecting their own preferences: if they had a taste for purple and gold houses, there would be no problem. The woman who wears hair curlers in the supermarket does not have to look at them while she benefits from their effects; the people around her gain no benefits but do have to look at them. Suppose we succeeded in imposing a rule that prevented anyone from wearing hair curlers in supermarkets. Instead of the woman with the curlers imposing her values on others, we would have the others imposing their preferences on her, and we would still be in a trap. What makes consumer externality traps so hard to avoid is the fact that they all incorporate a conflict of interest as their essential ingredient. In principle, the unpleasantness which Peter has imposed upon his fellows with his taste in dress could be countered by enforcing a conservative dress code, but this would leave us in the same sort of trap because of the pain which his fellows would then have imposed on him. In the same way, a driver who has arrived at the mattress in the middle of a road could be forced to get out and move it, but only at the cost of an additional inconvenience which has to be imposed on him in order to benefit everybody else on the road. It is intriguing to speculate why most people seem to regard the style-of-dress trap as an example of an unimportant social problem (or no problem at all), while the mattress problem looms as an unpleasant instance of self-interest dominating the public interest. Qualitatively, the situations are identical, and there is certainly no psychological support for a view that the unhappiness produced by a traffic jam is somehow greater than that produced by an offensive environment.

Production Externalities

A steel mill produces two different products—various kinds of steel and various forms of environmental pollution. These are not produced in strict proportions; the amount of pollution emitted depends not only upon total steel production, but also upon the effort expended on cleaning the production process and on limiting the uncontrolled disposal of wastes, and these are all matters of managerial policy. The reinforcement structure which guides the managers in these decisions is quite different from that faced by the public at large, however, and that is what leads into a trap. The market, which is the main source of rewards to steel mills, provides a high price for steel, reflecting the high value of steel to its users. On the other hand, there is no market where one can sell pollution control, and thus there are no managerial incentives that reflect the large punishments which waste products impose on the general population. Naturally, then, production managers learn to produce pollution in too high a ratio to the amount of steel, and the society is in a trap.

Although more subtle, a similar trap would exist even if it were impossible to vary the ratio of pollution to steel. Suppose that the technology of steel production were such that every ton of steel output necessarily was accompanied by some given decline in environmental quality, so that the only way to reduce pollution would be to reduce steel production. In this case, the total cost of the mill's output of steel has two components: the cost of the labor, machinery, and raw materials used in the manufacturing process, plus a cost reflecting the discomfort which the accompanying pollution imposes on the public at large. Nevertheless an individual consumer who buys products made with the steel only pays the cost of the physical resources because those are the only manufacturing inputs which are reflected in the market. Since these comprise only a part of the total social resource cost of steel, the product is priced improperly, and an excessive quantity will be used. In effect, the user of steel obtains it at too low a price. These purchases then impose a pollution punishment upon others (as well as upon the purchaser himself) and this is the externality trap again.

In practice, cases of industrial pollution involve both versions of the pollution trap. Production managers do not take steps to reduce the ratio of pollution to output (there are no rewards to them for doing so) and consumers do not pay the full social cost of the products which they buy.

In appearance, such production traps are similar to consumer-externality traps in that one individual—the manufacturer—seems to be imposing costs upon everyone else, but there is an important difference. Whereas consumer traps arise from differences in taste (or differences in position in a queue), pollution traps are produced by a simple failure in the market-reward system. In fact, production traps can arise even if everybody in the society has identical tastes. Ecologists and laymen often describe the pollution problem in terms of a simple antagonism between manufacturer and the general public, as though the manufacturer had some natural reason, inherent in his position as a producer, for disregarding the public interest. "Excessive" pollution is not basic to the technology of production, however; it is only a reflection of the fact that no one has bothered to see to it that the producers' rewards are made to reflect properly the public welfare. If the rewards to the producer were modified, the trap would go away, the manufacturers, as individuals, would be just as well off as they are now, and the general public would be better off.

We suspect that the antagonism so often observed between ecological interests and producer interests is not a reflection of the production trap in which market signals are simply inadequate guides to behavior, but derives instead from a more subtle consumer-externality trap, characterized by divergences in individual preferences. Retaining our example of steel production, there are those in our society who care relatively little for the uses of steel—the automobiles, the consumer durables, the bridges and office buildings—but who care a great deal about the air they breathe and the water they swim in. Others (apparently) take great joy in their new automobiles, their dishwashers, their snowmobiles, and their air conditioning, and to acquire these they are more than willing to put up with the polluted water and air which goes with them. Members of these two groups will have opposite opinions as to whether we should escape the trap by incorporating the full social cost of production into the prices of steel-made products. Any steps which we take in this direction will act to favor one group relative to the other: those individuals who enjoy consumption of durables, and who are not particularly offended by pollution prefer the present market system as it stands, because it leads to a pattern of rewards to steel producers which correspond to the preferences of these consumers themselves. From their point of view, there is no trap. The conservationists, on the other hand, are not content with the present trade-off between production and pollution, and they may even advocate the total elimination of pollution by law, because this would lead the steel manufacturers to behave in a manner which corresponds to their own personal tastes. Since no one likes to admit to antisocial behavior, and since adjustment to new sets of rewards and punishments may be temporarily unpleasant, the manufacturers themselves are likely to take part in these debates (on the side of the *status quo*), but logically they are not proper participants at all: the issue is the nature of the reward system which will lead producers into socially desirable patterns of behavior, and as long as they are rewarded for *something,* their long-run welfare is not particularly affected by the outcome.

Ways Out

We are aware of only a few general classes of opinion which seem to arise in response to externality traps. The first, particularly common to consumer-externality situations, is to deny that any trap exists. For example, it might be argued that Peter's outlandish style of dress irritates his co-workers only because they maintain outdated, intolerant attitudes. In effect, this view holds that Peter's co-workers have been no more wronged by his taste in clothes than they have by a spate of inclement weather, and that if they are offended, it is their own problem. Following similar reasoning, most people seem to believe that any driver has a "right" to obstruct traffic on a hill or to speed around a mattress, and that any more public-spirited behavior is to be appreciated as an unnecessary and unexpected courtesy. Such an attitude only obscures the problem since it refuses to admit the legitimacy of some people's preferences. In fact, a tradition of indifference toward certain kinds of personal taste may well lead to a belief that those preferences do not even exist. For readily comprehensible economic reasons, urban office buildings emphasize utility and economy at the expense of architectural grace. Occasional complaints that by accepting these economic considerations we have doomed ourselves to urban life in ugly, barren surroundings are dismissed as "unrealistic," that is, as reflecting only the preferences of an unimportant minority. We see the problem quite differently: there is a great technical difficulty in introducing aesthetic values into the marketplace for buildings because the benefits of good architecture do not accrue so much to those who pay for them as they do to the general public. In addition, of course, there are enormous quantitative difficulties in measuring the values which might be met. It does not follow from this, however, that these values are unimportant, but only that it is hard to translate them into reward systems which will encourage builders to make expenditures to enhance others' aesthetic enjoyment. Builders, seeing that architectural quality has no influence upon their own personal welfare, conclude that architectural quality is genuinely unimportant, and the society is in a trap.

Converting the Trap to a Trade-off

When confronted by simple externality situations, economists have almost invariably focused upon conversion of the trap into a trade-off as a resolution for the problem. After all, if a particular action is taken because someone's welfare is not reflected in the reward system of decision maker, the natural thing to do is to revise that reward system until it does more accurately reflect existing preferences. The application of this principle to production traps is quite straightforward. In the case of the polluting manufacturer, for example, the tradeoff technique would operate by having the company pay for the pollution which it produces; this could be accomplished by simply levying a tax on the emission of pollutants. From the producer's point of view, there is now a "market" for pollution reduction just as there is for steel, and he will no longer face reinforcers which reflect only a limited segment of more general social values. In the event that pollution cannot be reduced below some minimum level without prohibitive cost, some tax will still have to be paid; this will increase the cost of steel, and ensure that steel users will pay for the social cost which their consumption generates. When such pollution taxes are proposed, one occasionally hears objections which assert that the taxes will merely be "passed on" to consumers. In part, of course, that is precisely the outcome which we desire: unless the taxes are passed on, those who indirectly cause pollution by consuming products whose manufacture entails some environmental destruction are paying only part of the cost of their consumption behavior. Whether the tax raises the cost of steel significantly would depend on the nature of the technology. If the ratio of pollution to production is relatively easy to vary through technical adjustments, management will be led to avoid the tax by avoiding pollution. In the extreme case in which waste emissions are rigidly proportional to output, the tax will raise prices and force consumption to fall to a level more consistent with its real cost. In either case, the trap is resolved through replacement by a trade-off.

It may seem surprising that such a direct solution to a widely recognized problem should not have been implemented long ago. In part, we believe, this may be due to a failure to distinguish between the conflict and production components of the trap, permitting resentment over consumer externalities to prevent the resolution of production externalities. Thus even those individuals who agree that the quantity of pollution in the air and in the waters should be reduced see two opposite means for achieving this end: taxing the pollution emission as we have just suggested, or subsidizing the installation of pollution control devices in industrial plants. In practice, the first alternative is widely seen as antibusiness and the second as probusiness. In fact, however, although either method would reduce pollution, only one would resolve the trap. Subsidization of pollution control devices does not restore the trade-off which exists among the three elements, pollution, production, and cost, but only conceals it further. Such subsidies only make the product seem cheaper than it really is, and consumers of the product will not bear the cost of the pollution (or the pollution control) which is concomitant with their consumption. Instead, the cost of the pollution control is borne by everyone in society, whether they consume a great deal of the output of the manufacturer or not. The society as a whole is left in its trap, producing more than it should, and the subsidy simply spreads the burden of the trap indiscriminately among taxpayers.

There is a second common objection to these proposals. Even if there were no differences among people, and each of us viewed industrial pollution in exactly the same way, we would have to discover how to translate our values into a specific trade-off. It is sometimes argued that it is so difficult to obtain an accurate quantitative index of the social cost of pollution that the whole procedure should be abandoned as infeasible and an alternative sought. To our way of thinking, this argument loses its force once it is recognized that these alternative methods for dealing with the problem are all inferior to any reasonable approximation to plausible trade-off values. Indeed, most such alternatives turn out to be equivalent to the most extreme values of a pollution tax. If we make pollution entirely illegal, we in effect impose an enormously high tax, which may result in a disastrously sharp cutback in production—far more than the burdens of the pollution would ever justify. Alternatively, if we do nothing at all, or subsidize pollution control devices, that is equivalent to a zero tax on pollution, and leaves us enmeshed in the trap. It is surely better to make even rough estimates of the proper values for a tax than to fall back on one of these extremes. After all, once we have agreed that pollution is bad, we ought to be able to come up with some notion of how bad, and having done so, implementation of the resulting estimate would certainly be better than pretending that it is not bad at all (as the existing market prices suggest) or that it is infinitely bad (as outright prohibition of pollution would suggest).

Converting the trap to a trade-off is the economist's conventional solution to externality traps, and in the case of pure production traps, use of this procedure has never been seriously questioned. When consumer externalities enter in, however, the traditional form of the trade-off mechanism is not so compelling, and each new look at the problem leaves one less sure than before that conversion into a trade-off is even possible.

The conventional trade-off solution to consumer externalities would proceed as follows. Suppose that Mr. Brown, having read all about traps and trade-offs, says to Mr. Green, "I dislike that pea-green pin-stripe jacket of yours so much that your wearing it makes me feel as much worse off as would the loss of $20," and Mr. Green replies, "I like this jacket so much that I would have been willing to pay $10 more than its actual price to get it." That this describes a trap is clear. Purchase of the jacket imposes a $10 net loss on the two men in the aggregate. Moreover, conversion into a trade-off appears to be quite simple: Mr. Brown could pay Mr. Green $15 not to buy such a jacket and each would be better off by the equivalent of $5. Mr. Brown has only lost $15 instead of suffering the $20 equivalent loss. Mr. Green has gained $15 instead of the $10 equivalent benefit from paying for and wearing the jacket. This is an example of the sort of compensation criterion which economists traditionally have used to evaluate the relative desirability of alternative allocations of resources.

There are different methods for introducing a trade-off into Mr. Green's decision to buy the jacket, and these have different impacts upon the relative well-being of our two protagonists. Suppose that Mr. Green could not legally wear the jacket without Mr. Brown's approval, and this he could not get without paying $20 to Mr. Brown to compensate him for his loss. Again the trap is resolved (the jacket is not purchased), but Mr. Green is much worse off under this arrangement than he was under the first resolution (he has lost the $10 equivalent benefit from the jacket instead of gaining a new benefit of $5). A third means of resolution would arise if Mr. Green used the jacket as a threat—demanding $20 from Mr. Brown as a condition that the jacket not be worn. Again the trap is resolved, but now Mr. Brown loses $20 no matter what happens. Which of these alternatives applies is essentially a matter of law and culture. If Mr. Green has an established right to buy himself a jacket, however much it offends the sensibilities of his neighbors, then Mr. Brown has no choice but to pay a bribe if the trap is to be avoided. The mere existence of the pea-green pin-stripe jacket has produced a transfer of income from Mr. Brown to Mr. Green. On the other hand, if behavior which harms others, even in this relatively intangible way, is regarded as essentially antisocial, then Mr. Green must forego the benefits of something which would give him pleasure (or its monetary equivalent). Examples of each situation are readily available in our own society: whereas I have a right to paint my house in any color or pattern I choose (barring outright obscenity), I do not have a right to play my stereo loudly at four o'clock in the morning. Thus my neighbors will have to bribe me if they want me to live in a white house, but I have to bribe them if I want to listen to Beethoven.

At first glance, the trap-resolving potential of the trade-off resolving bribe seems quite neat. The difficulty with this approach is that the conflict of interest which characterizes consumer externality traps also interferes with the valuation which is necessary if the trap is to be converted into a trade-off. For example, what is to prevent Mr. Green from overstating the pleasure which he obtains from his jacket, in order to exact a bribe from Mr. Brown which is larger than necessary? Indeed, what if Mr. Green never intended to buy the jacket at all (actually, he doesn't like it either), but only proposed the purchase in order to frighten Mr. Brown into paying him off? Alternatively, if we were to modify our social code so that Mr. Green was required to compensate Mr. Brown for his suffering, what is to prevent Mr. Brown from overstating his losses so as to increase his income in the event that the jacket is purchased?

The incentive to misrepresent one's own preferences whenever an attempt is made to use payment schemes to resolve consumer externality traps is known among economists as the "revelation problem." Recognition of this defect has been effective in preventing any serious attempts to use trade-off inducing bribes to resolve these traps. In chapter 8, we will argue that it is not the trade-off device which is at fault, but a legal system which stresses compensation to the victims of externality traps: if Mr. Green has to pay Mr. Brown for his (Brown's) suffering, Mr. Brown is in effect being paid to exaggerate his losses, and, quite naturally, that is what he will do. As things stand, we must look elsewhere for escapes.

The problem of evaluating consumer-externality traps sometimes goes beyond the simple equity question of deciding who has the right to a benefit. Since the choice between alternative trade-offs influences the overall level of economic well-being enjoyed by Mr. Brown and Mr. Green, the quantitative (that is, dollar) evaluations of either damage done or pleasure gained from the green pin-stripe jacket may well depend upon the distributive choice which is made. Even the determination as to whether a trap exists may be influenced by the particular trade-offs which are selected. Suppose that it is established that all individuals have a right to consume whatever they like whenever they like without regard for the aesthetic costs imposed upon others. Mr. Brown, a sensitive and cultured man, has been forced to purchase heavy acoustic insulation to protect himself from noise, has been paying out of his own pocket to improve the appearance of his neighborhood, and for his emotional health, has built himself a retreat in the mountains. So expensive are these endeavors that he has trouble paying even for his own food and shelter. He may now admit that Mr. Green's jacket only makes him $5 worse off, not because it offends him less but because money has now become so scarce to him that he can no longer afford more than $5 for his bribe. So far as the jacket purchase is concerned, there is no longer a trap: Mr. Green benefits more from his jacket than Mr. Brown loses.

Obviously, one way to avoid traps which are caused by simple differences in preferences is to avoid contact with people who have significantly different patterns of tastes. This is perhaps a simple explanation for segregated living patterns. The evolution of such segregation is easy to visualize—those persons who are adversely affected through consumption externalities will simply relocate themselves where they will be free from the influence of the trap. As a long run consequence, people with similar tastes will be inclined to live and work together, isolating themselves from exposure to those whose habits or tastes are offensive to them. Moreover, once such homogeneous groups are established, their common backgrounds and common interests will decrease the likelihood that heterogeneous elements will enter the community because of the cumulative externalities which would then be imposed upon the newcomers.

Reinforcement Learning for Trap Escapes

Much of our emphasis upon reinforcement learning has dealt with the role which it plays in leading persons into traps; if reinforcers are properly established, however, we can learn our way out of traps just as well. This we believe can be a significant solution to consumer externality situations. From earliest childhood, reinforcers arise which encourage behavior beneficial to others and which punish activities harmful to others. Just as children can be rewarded for generosity toward family and playmates, so adults can be rewarded for trap-avoiding behavior. On appropriate occasions, Peter's neighbors can compliment him on his neatly trimmed lawn or on his new conservative tie and thereby encourage activity which is more consistent with general well-being. Obviously, this is the main defense we all use against the "thoughtless" behavior of others. We express appreciation for generosity and condemn overt self-interest, and the resulting learning will prevent the creation of an externality.

What is not so obvious but much more important is that trap-avoiding behavior learned in one context can be generalized to others. Peter's neighbors can compliment him on his lawn specifically or they can compliment him on the fact that he has taken an action which benefits the group. In the first case, the learning is confined to the lawn alone, and Peter is encouraged only to keep his grass trim and green; in the second, the learning is generalized to all activities which affect the neighborhood in general, so that Peter is not only encouraged to maintain his lawn, but to avoid other externality traps as well. Every child at some time or other is asked "to be considerate of others," that is, to avoid consumer externality traps, and if the lesson is learned well, a wide range of traps will be prevented whether or not specific instances of them have occurred before. The way, in short, to avoid consumer-externality traps is to use the reinforcement mechanism to encourage a general pattern of behavior rather than merely to punish specific instances of ignoring the welfare of others.

This generalized response to consumer externality situations is often made considerably easier by their symmetry. Mr. Green may be as offended by Mr. Brown's saddle shoes as is Mr. Brown by Mr. Green's jacket. Those who are considering admitting their friends into the front of a queue (giving "cuts") might remember that they themselves at some time will be at the end of a line. In these cases, it is possible to abstract from a specific trap at a specific place and time, and look at the problem in more general terms, visualizing ourselves in either of the two possible roles at one time or another; hence it becomes much easier to formulate general standards of conduct and introduce them into behavior. If behavior evolves from interpersonal experience in which role reversals are common, then a kind of cooperative behavior can develop in which, by common consent, externality traps are so avoided. Aesop's Fables are filled with morality tales stressing reversals and the importance of refraining from actions which harm others if one wants others to refrain from actions which harm oneself. Perhaps the best-known expression of this rule of symmetry is found in the Golden Rule's "Do unto others as you would have them do unto you." This invites us to imagine the impact of our externalities upon others as a guide to our own actions. This procedure, incidentally, is unavailable to production traps, since these are essentially asymmetric in the parts played by the manufacturer and the general public: the steel producer generates the pollution which affects others, but there is no circumstance in which consumers, so to speak, are in a position to impose pollution on the producer.

Superordinate Authority

Persons finding themselves victimized in an externality trap may often have recourse to the legal remedies available in a court of law. These remedies most typically take the form of a monetary payment from the offender to the offended in an amount intended to provide restitution for any damages suffered. Alternatively, an injunctive remedy may be sought which is designed to prevent future injuries by forbidding the continuation of the offending (externality-generating) behavior. Unfortunately, these remedies are frequently seriously deficient. Rather than restoring trade-offs, the usual procedure is to determine who has the "right" to impose on whom. Peter has the right to offend his neighbors' eyes by painting his house purple and gold, but not the right to offend their ears by playing his stereo at full volume at four o'clock. In this sense, the law rarely solves the problem, but only determines how its costs are to be distributed.

Sometimes steps are taken to enforce what someone imagines the outcome would be were the underlying trade-offs actually in force. For example, we are now witnessing a proliferation of pollution control "standards" which are intended to balance the costs imposed by the pollution against the realities imposed by existing technology. These are not trade-offs but only the results of a sort of public bargaining process between manufacturers who insist that pollution control is too expensive (if not impossible), and their opponents who demand that waste emissions be reduced to zero. The resulting standards are clumsy and are frequently tailored better to resolve political conflict than to resolve traps. They may even create new traps through the introduction of new reinforcement systems which are no better than the old. For example, automobile-emission standards have been formulated in terms of the fraction of noxious gases which are to be permitted in total exhaust. There is no evidence that those who imposed these standards realized that there are two ways to reduce a ratio: decrease the numerator or increase the denominator. These standards consequently led not to a reduction in total emissions, but to an increase in gasoline consumption, which, besides providing the energy necessary to lower pollution, increased the volume of exhaust against which the volume of pollutants was to be compared. Compared to the ensuing confusion over pollution, cost, and fuel consumption, a simple tax on the emissions would surely have been far simpler, less likely to create problems of its own, and far more consistent with our actual wishes.

7 *Stampedes*

Civil War

George Grosz
ink drawing 1930

The most outrageous
externality trap arises
when we begin blowing
one another up, yet the
entrapping ingredients
are readily apparent:
no party to such
foolishness has any
doubts that what he or
she is doing is justified
by the circumstances.

In the early morning of March 13, 1964, the residents of a New York apartment building were disturbed by cries and calls for help from the street outside their building. From their windows, they witnessed a young woman being assaulted by an unknown attacker. The scene, accentuated by the victim's cries for help, continued for several minutes before the attacker went away. After his departure, the woman, too seriously injured to enter the apartment building on her own, remained in the street continuing her cries for help, still without receiving any assistance. After some time, the attacker returned, the assault was renewed, and in a short time her neighbors became witnesses, not just to brutality, but to murder. Later, the victim was identified (her name: Kitty Genovese), and it turned out that her desperate situation and her appeals for help were evident to thirty-eight witnesses watching through their windows, yet none made any move to intervene, to assist, or even to call the police.

City officials and the public media reacted with shock and outrage, not to the fact of Kitty Genovese's death (after all, this sort of thing occurs daily in a large metropolis) but to the passive behavior of so many witnesses. Residents of the neighborhood were therefore closely questioned, but the explanations the witnesses gave for their inaction were quite simple. They said that they did not go directly to the aid of the victim because they were afraid of suffering the same fate and becoming victims themselves, or they said that they did not telephone the police for fear of becoming "involved," perhaps singled out for intensive interrogation by police, and certainly subject to revenge on the part of the killer or his friends. Ironically, at the time of the assault most witnesses did not feel much guilt for their inaction. Most had an expectation that some other witness would have greater initiative or more courage, and would come to the victim's aid or call for assistance. In short, each onlooker remained passive, not from indifference, but from fear compounded by the hope and expectation that someone else would pay the price of involvement.

The Kitty Genovese scandal is an instance of a simple extension of an externality trap. Any one of the witnesses could have taken an action which would have benefited not only Kitty Genovese but, indirectly, all the residents of the neighborhood. This action could have been taken, however, only at the cost of involvement and of increased personal risk, and evidently this cost was perceived to be larger than the private benefit of coming to the assistance of one in need. As a generalized form of externality trap, this example retains the property that the participants' interests are partially antagonistic. Despite a common concern, each individual would prefer that someone else play the martyr and call the police, and this led into the trap.

Nevertheless, this example differs from ordinary externality traps in that it is genuinely collective: no single individual can be pinpointed as the "cause" of the problem, and everyone is equally to blame. Whereas simple externality traps always arise because of the action or inaction of some identifiable party (such as the management of a steel mill or the person at the head of a queue), the Kitty Genovese trap arose from universal inaction for which everyone shared the responsibility. This being the case, one might imagine that a collective trap such as this would be easier to avoid than would simple externality traps, because with a larger number of possible actors there is much greater chance of finding someone among them who might be willing to perform the necessary service. That just the reverse is often the case was indicated by the testimony of witnesses to Kitty Genovese's death: each witness was less inclined to action because of the belief that someone else would call the police. It was the very fact that the number of potential actors was large that led each to believe that his or her individual sacrifice was not necessary. If there had been only one resident of the neighborhood who had a telephone, it would have been obvious to everyone who should call the police, and we have the paradoxical result that with only one rather than many telephones available, Kitty Genovese's life might have been saved.

This surprising conclusion that one's chances of receiving

assistance from bystanders decreases as the number of bystanders increases has become the subject of considerable social science research. A number of studies which have been
conducted in the psychological laboratory and in field settings
have provided formal experimental support to supplement the
anecdotal evidence of this phenomenon. Apparently, the dif-
fusion of responsibility which occurs when large numbers of
persons are present obscures the obligation which each might
feel toward another in need of assistance; thus one is more
likely to drown unaided at a crowded beach than at one which
is sparsely populated, or a hitchhiker may have better luck on
a lightly traveled road than upon a major freeway.

The study of collective traps has been underway, in one
form or another, for many years. One of the earliest applications of the principle arose when economists recognized that
business firms, following their own individual self-interests,
would reap smaller profits than could be generated if they
were to formulate a collective pricing policy and put it into
practice. From a social point of view, of course, such coordination (amounting to monopoly) is generally undesirable, since
it would lead to overcharging consumers, but from the individual points of view of the businessmen themselves, their
uncoordinated profit-oriented behavior leads only to collectively lower profits. It is interesting to observe that here is a
case of a trap which is actually socially beneficial: in the interests of obtaining market prices which will accurately reflect
production costs, economists are strongly inclined to support
policies which will help keep businessmen *in* this trap rather
than helping them out of it.

The desire that individual business interests be required to
pursue their "self-interest" without the advantage of cooperative collusion is implemented through the enactment and enforcement of anti-trust legislation intended to prevent the sort
of "cooperation" in the commercial sphere which we, as a
society, generally attempt to foster in other spheres of social
activity. It is the pursuit of individual self-interest which produces littered parks and playfields, the wasteful consumption

of scarce resources, and the death of Kitty Genovese. Certainly in these latter instances, what we seek are devices to promote the *common* interests as against self-interest, some social device which will motivate us to engage in a form of "collusion" which by benefitting the collective also benefits the individuals which comprise it.

Economists, in another capacity, have encountered collective traps in the provision of what are usually called "public goods." These are commodities which more or less benefit everyone in a society when they are made available, and common examples are schools, hospitals, fire departments, law courts, public health programs, and the like. Suppose that the construction of a new hospital is proposed, with the necessary funding to be raised through public subscription. The trap arises because the quality of the facility is not likely to be affected noticeably by the size of any individual donor's contribution to the building fund, although it is certainly affected by the aggregation of individual donations. Just as everyone in Kitty Genovese's apartment building assumed that someone else would call the police and that additional calls were unnecessary, so Peter, recognizing that his own donation will be insignificant in the aggregate and have no substantial effect on the building of the hospital, may conclude that a large contribution on his part is unnecessary and consequently donate less than he otherwise would. If many people follow Peter's reasoning, each giving less than the hospital is worth to them on the principle that the provision of the hospital is not contingent on their individual donations, the fund may prove to be inadequate for any hospital at all, and the society is in a collective trap. Economists have traditionally viewed this as the most likely outcome of any attempt to provide public goods through voluntary contributions, and they have therefore usually advocated the use of government taxing power to assure that appropriate quantities of such collectively useful goods will be acquired.

These "public goods" traps are often believed to be the unavoidable consequences of "individually rational" behavior and therefore to require third party intervention by a super-ordinate authority. Yet, the possibility that the victims them-selves can escape these traps in at least some cases has been made clear in another context. Recently, social scientists have been experimenting extensively with behavior in situations in-volving the so-called Prisoner's Dilemma, a simple two-person paradigm first described by the mathematician A. W. Tucker. The prisoner's dilemma is described by the following scenario: Two persons suspected of bank robbery have been captured by the police and are found to be carrying concealed weapons. The two are isolated from one another, and each is presented with the following offer by the prosecuting attorney. If neither con-fesses to bank robbery, both will be imprisoned for two years on a concealed weapons charge. If one turns "state's evidence," implicating the other in the robbery, he will be released, while the other will in all likelihood be convicted and sentenced for twenty years. If both confess to bank robbery, then of course both must be imprisoned as robbers, but for "only" about ten years, a lesser sentence to reflect the fact that both gave infor-mation to the authorities. These conditions are commonly rep-resented by means of a diagram as shown below:

		Prisoner 2	
		Confess	Do Not Confess
	Confess	Prisoner 1: 10 years Prisoner 2: 10 years	Prisoner 1: 0 years Prisoner 2: 20 years
Prisoner 1	Do Not Confess	Prisoner 1: 20 years Prisoner 2: 0 years	Prisoner 1: 2 years Prisoner 2: 2 years

One can see from the diagram that each prisoner is better off if he "confesses" no matter which alternative is taken by the other: if the other confesses, the first avoids ten additional years in prison by confessing himself; if the other does not confess, the first avoids a sentence of two years by turning state's evidence. (It is an incidental yet an interesting feature of this problem that these conditions are unaffected by whether or not the two are actually guilty of robbing the bank!) The nature of the trap is clear: if both prisoners obey the logic of the situation, then both will confess and each will be imprisoned for ten years, and yet if neither had confessed, each would have been imprisoned for only two years, a substantially shorter time. In principle, the prisoners face the same dilemma which concerns two businessmen competing in the same market: at a high price each would profit most by producing a larger amount of output, but if both attempt to increase sales, the price will be depressed and the profits of both firms will be reduced. In each example, an individual (prisoner or businessman) following his own private interests (short prison term or profits) does less well than he would if all individuals coordinated their behavior for the sake of collective gains.

As an experimental paradigm the Prisoner's Dilemma has attracted far more attention among social scientists than has the much older economic model, possibly because it emphasizes that despite its compelling logic, the competitive alternative (both prisoners confessing) is not a behavioral necessity. The outcome which results when individually rational behavior is the guideline is so obviously inappropriate from the standpoint of group welfare that one must wonder if people can be taught to avoid such traps as a general matter. Some research reported in the psychological literature suggests that trap-avoiding behavior is fairly common: subjects in Prisoner's Dilemma situations who are unknown to one another, who are to encounter the problem only once, and who are guaranteed anonymity (to avoid the possibility of future reprisals for non-cooperative behavior), nevertheless frequently choose a cooperative (group gain) rather than a competitive (self-gain) action as a matter of course, despite the apparent rationality behind the opposite choice. These experiments are usually performed using small payoffs—a few cents worth of gain or loss—rather than the much larger values found in real-world situations, and one might therefore object that the results may be confined to small-reward traps. Whether or not this view is justified, the principle is nevertheless established that cooperative behavior is frequently carried over into situations which themselves offer no inducement for it.

Iterative Traps

The Prisoner's Dilemma was originally proposed as a single-instance situation, a discrete interpersonal transaction not to be repeated. One might imagine the prisoners to have been strangers until shortly before the bank robbery and to have no plans or expectations of further communications afterward. Under such circumstances, there is no interaction between the prisoners beyond the immediate problem. This limitation is essential to the conclusion that confession is "rational"; if the two prisoners are instead regular partners in crime, or if there is some way in which an agreement to cooperate can be enforced, such as some established system of retributive justice for criminals which punishes those who turn in their accomplices, then it may not be true that confession is the best strategy, because it may bring about severe future punishments or the loss of future rewards. In general, the more often a trap of this type repeats itself with the same participants confronting one another, the more likely it is that the situation will afford to each the opportunity to inflict future retribution upon the other in exchange for uncooperative behavior. With repetition of the trap, it is even possible for the participants to develop elaborate contingent strategies: "whatever my partner (or adversary, depending upon one's attitude toward the situation) does in this instance, I will imitate on the next occasion." The pattern of behavior which results from such resolutions can quickly lead out of the trap into cooperation, even in the absence of any explicit communication beyond the choice behavior itself.

When there are only a few participants, and the trap is repeatedly occurring, contingent strategies can lead to escape, but it is obvious that the effectiveness of these self-help strategies is reduced when the number of people who are participants in the same trap increases. Suppose that my neighbor and I share an isolated enclave, and that he mows his lawn in the summer so infrequently that I suffer from its unsightliness. Knowing that he values neatness as much as I, and fails to cut his grass largely because he is lazy, I institute a practice of mowing my own lawn immediately after he mows his and otherwise not at all. The consequence of this policy of contingent mowing is that my neighbor finds his own efforts to be much more gratifying—whenever he mows, two lawns get trimmed instead of only one, and the neighborhood is made doubly attractive as a result. If this added incentive is sufficient to overcome his lassitude, we are both better off. Suppose instead that we live not in an isolated enclave but in a neighborhood of many adjacent homes. If the entire neighborhood is inhabited by lazy neighbors, the contingency mowing strategy will lose its effectiveness. If I mow immediately after *anyone* mows, then my lawn may be constantly so neat that the difference is scarcely noticeable. If I direct my attentions to only a few neighbors, the effects are still badly dissipated: what difference does it make if 10 percent of the surrounding lawns are trimmed in response to one's own mowing while the others remain unaffected?

Experimental studies of behavior in Prisoner's Dilemma situations support this view that escape from the trap becomes increasingly difficult as the number of participants becomes large: subjects in two-person iterative experiments usually manage eventually to coordinate their behavior and avoid the trap even when they are unable to communicate with one another other than by their actual choices in the "game." When similar experimental situations are run with seven or more participants, the development of a cooperative coordination becomes almost impossible to achieve. In a similar vein, economists frequently use the number of major producers in a market as an index of its "competitiveness," in effect, as an index of the difficulty which member firms will face in escaping from their own trap. In the economic example, this increase in difficulty seems to take place in spite of the fact that these market traps also are likely to involve greater losses to each participant as the number of participants increases. That is, individually rational behavior (competition) produces larger reductions in profit when the number of firms is large than when the number of firms is small, and one might expect this fact to lead to increased pressure to escape and develop a cooperative interaction.

The difficulties in reaching satisfactory outcomes when the number of participants is large was manifestly apparent in the Kitty Genovese case which we have already cited. It was clear from the testimony of witnesses that the large number of persons who were available to give her assistance actually contributed to the trap. The problem was undoubtedly compounded by the nature of the city in which they all dwelled. New York City contains millions of people, and the impersonality which such an environment breeds undoubtedly extends even to situations in which only a small number of persons are directly involved. Kitty Genovese was a stranger even to her immediate neighbors, and they indicated under questioning that this anonymity contributed to her plight. Some evidence of regional differences in helping behavior has been reported in the scientific literature. In a study by Latane and Dabbs (1975) in which an experimenter "accidentally" dropped containers of pencils in crowded elevators in various United States cities, it was observed that a southern gentleman was much more likely to come to the aid of a lady in distress than was his northern counterpart. Men in distress, however, were no more likely to receive help below than above the Mason-Dixon line.

The many-person collective trap appears frequently as a congestion problem. An old example of this is found in the practice of grazing sheep on a town common: the owner who adds a sheep to his own flock benefits fully from the growth and by-products of the extra sheep, but only shares in a small way in the cost imposed by the increased grazing. Even if the common affords insufficient food for the aggregate size of the community flock, an individually rational owner may still add more sheep because most of the costs (in the form of limits on food consumption) are imposed upon other sheep owners. The total flock, as a consequence, is likely to exceed the capacity of the common and the society of sheep growers is in a trap. This particular trap has recently been rediscovered by scientists concerned with problems of global overpopulation. Some, such as Garrett Hardin, actually go beyond the simple congestion result and argue that the flock will increase in size steadily through time, its ultimate size limited only by the total depletion of the available food supply. This extreme result, however, is not a logical consequence of congestion alone: as the commons is overutilized, even the private value of adding one additional sheep is correspondingly reduced. As the overutilization of the common increases, a point is reached where the rational owner will eventually find this value to be less than the cost of the sheep itself. Increases in the size of the flock beyond this point would occur only in the presence of a sliding-reinforcer trap: since the expansion of the size of one's own flock was in the past always desirable and successful, the process of expansion may become habitual and not be tempered until long after the resources of the common have been exhausted.

Congestion traps are an ordinary part of contemporary life. An obvious example is the traffic congestion which plagues every American city, surrounded by suburbs, whose access roads are generally clear except during rush hours between approximately seven and nine in the morning and between four thirty and six thirty in the afternoon. At five o'clock in the afternoon, every office worker in the city is faced by the same choice: whether to depart for home immediately (in which case one must suffer the slow pace, congestion, and frustration of the rush hour traffic), or to wait an hour or so, occupying that time as best one can in the city, and then depart when the worst of the traffic congestion is over. Since most workers are tired by five o'clock, have little to do in the city at that time and no wish to remain, everyone chooses to leave at five. In effect, each commuter weighs the costs of battling the traffic against the benefits of being home half an hour earlier (we assume the traffic jam increases driving time by about half an hour), and concludes that the benefits exceed the costs. Such a calculation, however, does not include the costs which each commuter imposes upon others. By going home at five, each commuter adds to the traffic and slows the progress of everyone else who is going home at five. As is the case in all consumer-externality traps, each commuter is seeing only a part of the actual trade-off which is concerned. The true total cost of the decision to leave at five includes both one's own inconvenience and the inconvenience which one imposes upon others, and these two together may sum to more than the benefits of being home half an hour earlier even if the private cost alone does not. Since each commuter must himself pay only the private cost, each commuter chooses to leave at five and everyone is made worse off. The situation is in principle identical to that faced by Kitty Genovese's neighbors or by the participants in a Prisoner's Dilemma experiment, except that the number of people involved in our traffic example is much larger and, consequently, their anonymity far greater.

Congestion traps occur in other contexts in which they may have more serious consequences than merely delaying one's arrival home after work. On very hot days in the eastern part of the United States, so many people operate air conditioners that the electric power system is overloaded and occasionally fails. Suppose the government were to launch a publicity campaign urging everyone to conserve power (by keeping buildings warmer, cooling only a few rooms, or operating air conditioners only part of the day). The incentive structure faced by individuals is identical to that found in the Prisoner's Dilemma example. If the government campaign is successful, and a power failure is avoided, each consumer of electricity may nevertheless conclude that had he disregarded the government's pleas for conservation and instead run his air conditioning at full power, his excessive consumption alone would not have been sufficient to overload the entire system, and his dwelling would have been even more comfortable. On the other hand, if the campaign is a failure and a blackout occurs, the individual user will still be more comfortable if he runs his own system as long as possible. Thus, whether or not the power fails, each individual is better off not conserving. The pattern of incentives which are presented to the individual by the structure of the electrical-distribution system will lead each to overconsume, overloading the system until everyone is denied electric power.

The difficulties caused by such an incentive structure are underlined when we consider what "lessons" are taught to the well-intentioned citizen who voluntarily complies with the government's request for conservation. If there is an electrical shutdown, the conclusion will be reached that the conservation effort was fruitless compounded by the realization that those who *didn't* comply with the conservation pleas at least enjoyed air conditioning up until the time of power failure. Alternatively, if there is no power failure, it appears that one's own compliance merely contributed to the comfort of those who ignored conservation. Thus, while some individuals may start off doing their share in conserving a scarce resource the feeling that "their share" is either too insignificant to matter or will be expropriated by others can reduce the ranks of the socially responsible, and future requests for conservation by public officials will serve as nothing more than the starting flag of a race to grab what one can before the well runs dry.

Our experience with the fifty-five-mile-an-hour speed limit on American highways is following this same pattern. Before the limit was made "mandatory" as a fuel conservation measure, an attempt was made to accomplish the same goal with a voluntary program. Initially, there was a relatively high degree of compliance. However, "cooperative" drivers traveling at fifty-five miles per hour soon realized that other drivers who passed them at higher speeds were consuming the very fuel that the slower drivers were making sacrifices to conserve. So, as with the air conditioning problem, the vast majority of drivers eventually concluded that they would rather be going at highway speeds when the gas ran out. Now, even the mandatory program is under attack as compliant drivers watch lawbreakers pass them by with impunity and realize that as before, their own sacrifices are only subsidizing others.

The list of such congestion traps is virtually endless. We are now threatened with the possibility of severe fuel shortages in winter. The day may come when fuel is not available for homes, schools and businesses during severe cold spells. If everyone were to keep his thermostat five degrees lower, enough fuel might be conserved to eliminate the shortage, and by sacrificing a bit of our personal comfort, we could keep these institutions operating during cold weather. Congestion in department stores at Christmas time is another example: each shopper finds it easier to put off gift shopping until just before Christmas rather than to plan ahead and carry out this task well in advance of the Christmas rush. (Of course, this bit of procrastinating behavior is the result of a time-delay trap— the bother of shopping is avoided by simply postponing it, leading to the greater future difficulties which last-minute shopping will impose.) In appraising the "convenience" of postponing shopping until the last minute, each individual fails to recognize or "add in" the cost which his own presence in the store imposes upon others. This individual calculus, ignoring the costs to others, underestimates the overall social cost and so the group is trapped.

Most people in our society understand the nature and causes of traffic jams and power shortages, but this understanding alone is hardly sufficient to remedy the problem. At the heart of the matter lies the fact that on an *individual basis* each of us is better off behaving in the very manner which catches the group up in the trap—if anything, when an individual comes to understand such a trap it accelerates the very behavior which produces the trap; knowing others will hoard wheat during a famine, the "rational" individual will try to get to the granary first.

In general, congestion traps arise whenever there are a great many people who wish to use a relatively scarce resource or limited facility all at the same time. The traffic jam is a consequence of limited roadways, the power shortage is a consequence of scarce gas, coal, and oil resources, and the Christmas shopping rush is a consequence of limited department store facilities and sales personnel. Of course, it is often possible to resolve these problems by expanding the associated facilities, but the expense may be absurdly high compared to other devices for solving the problem. Do we really want to expand our highway facilities for the sake of an hour's worth of traffic? If we spend millions of dollars building roads because we can find no means to coordinate the time of departure of office workers, then we may be in as much of a trap as ever. The construction of increased electric generation capacity is a very expensive way of avoiding a brief power shortage: it is comparable to a policy of constructing new department stores as a means for avoiding five days of holiday shopping congestion. Similarly, fuel resources can probably be supplemented with nuclear energy, but many feel that the use of nuclear power plants is too costly (that is, risky) to be justified by the occasional power shortage which it would allow us to avoid.

Ways Out

Most collective traps are characteristically easy to recognize, possibly because we are all victims at one time or another. Nothing can be more obvious that the tragedy of the Kitty Genovese situation, the hardships caused by electric or gas shortages, or the anger and frustration caused by traffic congestion, and it is a tribute to the subtlety and drawing power of these traps that they recur over and over again despite their ease of recognition. Unlike time-delay traps, ignorance traps, or sliding-reinforcer traps, in which a thorough understanding of the nature of the trap may itself be of great assistance in avoiding it, awareness of externality traps is often insufficient to bring about any sort of remedy.

Converting the Trap to a Trade-Off

Collective externality traps arise whenever individual decision makers face reinforcers which are inconsistent with the payoffs which the behavior imposes upon others: when individuals do not bear the whole cost of their actions, or do not see the whole benefit. The obvious procedure for dealing with traps of this type is the one which we have previously advocated for other traps, and that is to make the social trade-offs apparent to each individual. Although they are composed of externality situations, collective traps are essentially symmetric in that those who "cause" the externalities are also victims. The individual who "imposes" his automobile engine fumes upon the atmosphere can no more avoid breathing them than any other victim in the trap. By driving, he generates pollution which affects everyone, but by not driving, he still breathes the air polluted by others. Since, for the individual, the benefits of driving outweigh the increased cost imposed by adding one's own pollution to the total, the *individualistically* rational decision is to go on driving. Nevertheless, the total pollution is suffered by each individual, and we therefore are not faced by the fundamental conflict of interest which makes the development of an equitable trade-off so difficult in simple consumer externality traps. We are all in these traps together and should jointly benefit from their avoidance.

It is not necessary to imitate the economist and advocate only financial trade-offs when seeking remedies to collective traps; there are punishments other than taxes and rewards other than cash subsidies which can be used to guide behavior. In practice, however, monetary devices do possess an attractive flexibility. For example, in dealing with congestion problems, economists have for many years proposed as a solution the simple device of charging higher prices for use of the scarce resource during the peak period of congestion and then using the revenue obtained from those higher prices to expand capacity as much as that revenue will allow. One might, for example, deal with the traffic congestion problem by constructing toll booths on all roads leaving a central city and use the toll booths only during the rush hour. The toll charge would be designed to reflect the fact that during the rush hour, each commuter is imposing a cost on other people, and the toll therefore compels each commuter to evaluate the trade-off that confronts the society as a whole rather than the trade-off which formerly affected him alone. Similar techniques could be applied to our other examples. Many electric power companies in the United States are experimenting with electric meters which have been designed to record consumption during peak demand periods separately from that registered during off-peak periods, enabling lower prices to be charged during uncongested times. The higher price charged during peak hours can be considered to be a reflection of the higher social cost which use at critical times entails. The sophistication of this system is such that it would also be a simple matter to increase charges further during heat waves so as to reflect the high social cost imposed by those who, by operating their air conditioners at full power, are contributing to a power overload which is endangering the supply of electricity to everyone. This same device provides an index of the value of increased capacity: willingness to pay peak-load prices is equivalent to a willingness to pay for increases in the general availability of the resource.

To convert collective traps back into their essential and underlying trade-offs is potentially a simple and effective means for dealing with these situations. It is unfortunate that such remedial procedures, which have been recognized and understood for so many years, have so rarely been put into effect. In some instances, justification for this inaction may be found in the initial costs of installing the necessary hardware—the turnstiles, toll booths, timed electric meters, and so forth—but certainly these expenses are far smaller than the expenses which have been made in attempting to solve the problems by expanding resources to meet peak load demand. A classic example is found in the case of the New York City water supply. There are no water meters in use in Manhattan. Thus, anyone using water obtains all the rewards which the ready availability of water provides, yet at the same time, can remain blissfully unaware of its cost. The city of Manhattan is one of the few places in the world where, from the individual's point of view, it is actually cheaper to leave a faucet dripping or a toilet running continuously than it is to call the plumber to repair it. From the social point of view, of course, the plumber is cheaper. Not surprisingly, per capita water consumption in Manhattan is extraordinarily high, and the city has been forced to go to great expense to provide sufficient capacity to meet the public demand, an expense, moreover, which considerably exceeds the cost of installing a water meter in every dwelling in the city. The residents of the city, however, have apparently failed to recognize the connection between their collective water consumption and their collective tax bill, and continue to advocate the provision of "free" water.

Any proposal to convert a collective trap into a trade-off does require that one deal with a variety of objections which arise from a concern with equitable income distributions. An economic tax upon a scarce resource during a time of peak consumption is sometimes said to discriminate against the poor. It is argued, for example, that if we charge a toll on highways leaving the city, it will be the rich who get home by 5:15, while the poor will all be forced to wait an additional half hour. Similarly, the rich would be able to operate their air conditioning during heat waves while the poor could not afford it. The assumption of this argument that taxes would have a much greater effect upon the behavior of the poor than upon the rich (who also have other uses for their money) has never been properly documented, but quite apart from this, such an argument fails to recognize that the existence of the trap itself is not a function of income level: *anyone* driving home at five o'clock, be he rich or poor, imposes a cost on other people and such a person is using a scarce resource (in this case occupying limited space) in as genuine a sense as if he were consuming steel, housing, or agricultural produce. By not charging for the use of that resource, the rest of the members of society are, in effect, making a sacrifice equal to the cost of that resource. Moreover, it is possible to restore the trade-off, substituting it for the trap without discriminating against those with low incomes. Suppose that we did levy a tax which reflected traffic congestion costs, and then provided an equivalent lump-sum dollar grant to each commuter whose income fell below some specified level. The grant guarantees that the well-being of the poor commuter is not influenced by the tax, and we can be sure that he can now "afford" the payment. With respect to his ability to drive home when he likes, the poor commuter is now at least as well off as the rich, and one could not argue that establishing the trade-off discriminated against him. Even so, it does not follow that the poor commuter would continue to travel home at five o'clock: like everyone else, he has alternative uses for his money and he is quite likely to spend some of his grant in other ways, accepting as the price a later return to home. The point is that low-income individuals have difficulty purchasing goods and services because of their low income, not because those goods and services have particular costs attached to them as prices, and it does them no service to subsidize their incomes with specific goods (such as encouraging them to drive home at five o'clock) when they would perhaps much prefer to spend the equivalent value of resources on other things.

Most proposals which economists have made for trade-off-restoring taxes (or subsidies) have been insensitive to the question of income levels. Roughly speaking, when a resource is overused because of improper pricing, it is overused by both rich and poor. If taxing mechanisms are used to correct the problem, it is certainly possible (though not necessary) that the benefits and costs would be inequitably distributed among income classes. Compensation for such inequities may be a prerequisite to general acceptance of these proposals, and the proper design of such compensation is an important part of the design of any trap-avoiding program. Nevertheless, it would be absurd for us to permit a concern for income differentials to prevent the appropriate pricing of goods and services; that would just put us right back in the trap with our traffic jams, our power shortages, our over-heated houses, and all the rest, when we know full well that there exist patterns of behavior which would benefit everyone.

The Habit of Cooperation

Those who subscribe to cognitive models of behavior typically see externality traps as inevitable facts of life rather than merely potential threats to our social well-being. The logic of the Prisoner's Dilemma is so compelling that some social scientists accept the noncooperative outcome as a standard model of behavior. As corollaries to this rationalist view, one might conclude that public exhortations to the effect that we all take steps to conserve energy are pointless and have no hope of success, that fund-drives for hospitals and universities cannot be expected to generate contributions from any but those wealthy patrons who stand to reap benefits on their income tax returns, and that no one should have been surprised when Kitty Genovese failed to gain assistance from her neighbors. The fact that none of these statements is entirely correct—that some energy is being conserved, that not only the rich make contributions, and that we are shocked and indignant by the inaction of Miss Genovese's neighbors—suggests that we expect and receive some cooperation from one another as a matter of course.

Some indication of the underlying propensity and capacity of humans to establish and maintain cooperative interactions can be gleaned from the experimental studies of social behavior in the Prisoner's Dilemma situation. These experiments have demonstrated that even strangers can sometimes establish cooperative relationships in the face of temptations to seek individual benefits through competition with others. Commonly, these experiments employ an abstract matrix form such as the one in the following diagram:

		Person 2	
		A	B
Person 1	A	1, 1	−20, 20
	B	20, −20	−5, −5

In this table, the first number in each cell represents the payoff to person 1 and the second number represents the payoff to person 2. A particular cell is selected by the combination of individual choices made by the two persons. So for example, the lower left hand cell would determine the payoffs if person 1 were to choose row B and person 2 were to choose column A.

When presented with this "game," many people see choice B as "obviously" the "right" way to play, and it is only after many iterations that the choices of some shift to A. For a substantial number of people, the individually rational choice of B is so persistent that the shift to A is never accomplished at all, and the trap has closed forever. There are many others, however, who see choice A as "obviously" the "right" way to play from the outset, and they sometimes persist in that choice over several plays even if their opponents (potential partners) exploit them with repeated selections of B. The implication is inescapable that some persons bring with them behavioral habits which, had they been shared by other players, would have avoided the trap entirely, without any recourse to governmental coercion, tax or subsidy schemes, or even strategies involving conditional choice.

There is other evidence that collective traps can be avoided by their potential victims without any help or intervention from outside. The citizens of prerevolutionary Philadelphia often succeeded in providing themselves with schools and hospitals (archetypical public goods) through voluntary contributions, and this was done in the absence of any functioning centralized government. Harvard College was originally founded and supported entirely by public subscription. Recent water shortages in California have stimulated such dramatic conservation efforts that local water supply districts were unable to sell enough water to cover their own costs. Successful charity fund drives are a part of our everyday experience. The evidence is strong that it is possible for people to learn to behave cooperatively, and for that behavior to extend into novel situations. Ideal as this solution may be, it may not provide a long term answer to the problem. The reinforcers which are attached to the trap are not modified in any way, and there is great danger that some individuals will eventually succumb to it. When that happens, the pressures on others are increased and we expect more and more people to turn to the self-interested choices which drive the entire society into the trap.

8

Judicial and Legislative Escapes

With our fates in the hands of such as these. . . .

Most of our efforts up to this point have been directed toward the identification and description of the different types of social trap. At the same time, we have identified a number of specific techniques for avoiding traps or escaping from them. In general, these have been of two different types: those which rely upon individual actions on the part of those persons who are (potentially) trapped themselves, and those which involve more formal social action either through the courts or through the legislative process.

In preceding chapters the emphasis has been upon solutions or remedies that rely upon individual efforts and informal actions. This was because of our belief that it is a property of traplike situations that to be forewarned is to be forearmed. Many of the problems posed by traps are problems of self-awareness: one who is conscious of the dangers contained in time delays, intermittent reinforcers, and other traps is better prepared to take account of the potential punishments which may attach to one's behavior. In part, too, we have chosen not to emphasize solutions to traps which rely upon outside intervention, appeals to formal authority, or the coercive power of the state because these methods have an objectionably paternalistic flavor and tempt us to fall into the trap of telling others that we know better than they what constitutes their own best interests.

It would be unrealistic, however, to put all of our reliance upon consciousness-raising and self-help methods. We have already recognized that simple intellectual knowledge is frequently no match for the appeal of an immediately available tangible reinforcer, and it is evident that escapes from traps with external components demands not only awareness but a substantial degree of altruism as well. In this chapter, therefore, we turn to the second class of trap-avoiding procedures, concentrating on the effectiveness of legal systems in dealing with traps.

Legislative mechanisms and the law have historically been called upon to solve social problems which fall in all of the trap categories which we have identified. At the same time, the way in which these legal goals are pursued reveals implicit theories of human behavior, if only because it is impossible to devise solutions to any human problems without presupposing some behavioral and institutional structure for the problems themselves. If we examine the legal system and the methods which it uses to solve problems, these theories of behavior are exposed in a form which permits comparison with current scientific knowledge, and we can gain thereby some insight into the shortcomings of contemporary legal remedies, at the same time suggesting some more efficacious approaches to the same issues.

If we seek to find some consistent model of human behavior imbedded in our legal system, we are bound to be disappointed. In fact, the behavioral theories which might be inferred from our present sociolegal structure are astonishingly ambiguous. Our Internal Revenue Code incorporates tax credits for business investment which are defended on the grounds that they will stimulate growth. The same code provides extra deductions for larger families in order to ease the tax burden upon those who "happen" to have many children. Thus the same body of law implies the contradictory views that the investment credit changes behavior while the dependents' deduction does not. One might argue with equal logical persuasiveness that the investment tax credit conveys windfall profits to those firms which "happen" to be growing, while the dependents' deduction stimulates unwanted population growth!

Our criminal justice system apparently relies upon a belief that the threat of imprisonment will deter crime even though that punishment is both uncertain and delayed in time. In contrast, our welfare system provides support for female single-parent families, apparently without any consideration for the possibility that the severity of the welfare problem may be influenced by what is intended as its solution. With equal consistency, critics of these programs can maintain that, by neglecting the root causes of crime, the penal system is useless in altering criminal behavior, but that, by placing a premium upon single-parenthood, our welfare system is destroying otherwise stable families.

Such contradictions extend into purely economic areas: if we decide that we must increase the number of professional engineers in our society, we propose fellowship support for engineering students as an effort to make the choice of an engineering career easier, but few people have taken seriously existing quantitative estimates of the extent to which unemployment compensation influences the incidence of unemployment by altering the willingness of those who are unemployed to reject jobs which do not suit their tastes.

The list of such inconsistencies in our system of social legislation is endless. Our purpose in pointing them out, however, is not to demonstrate that all of these programs (or even half of them) are bad, but to point out how little consideration is typically given to analyzing and measuring the broad-ranging behavioral consequences of law. One might take the position that these contradictions have come about because legislators and the courts are wholly ignorant of the elements of human behavior, but this seems to be implausibly far-fetched. If asked, successful politicians and experienced judges would probably lay claim to a keener than average insight into others' behavior on the grounds that they share with bartenders and cabdrivers opportunities to observe their fellow man in circumstances more revealing of human nature than usual settings allow.

It seems to us that in spite of a desire to protect human rights, to identify the regions and limits of individual responsibility, and to guarantee minimal levels of personal well-being, the superficial and short-term aspects of social needs have been so pressing that our society has been inclined to overlook the importance of human motivation altogether. Certain reinforcers affect behavior only after the passage of time. When we concern ourselves only with this week's or next week's problems, we naturally give short shrift to behavioral consequences which will occur only much later. However, by taking such a myopic view of social problems, or by responding only to those aspects of problems which are of immediate concern, we have come to overlook the fact that this week's system of social policies creates a reinforcing environment which inevitably shapes next year's behavior, and that long-term changes in behavior are certain to follow changes in contemporary laws and policy.

What would be useful as a first step toward the resolution of traps at all levels is an increased awareness on the part of legislators and the courts of the dynamics of behavior shaping. It is particularly important that efforts be made to quantify the behavioral effects of legislative changes. It is natural that those who have strong political commitments on one side or the other of an issue are inclined to take extreme positions on these behavioral questions. The probusiness legislator praises investment tax credits as major stimuli to growth (and "job creation"); there are some people who regard the disincentive effects of unemployment compensation to be so overwhelming as to justify its abolition; and the "welfare-rights" supporter may refuse to acknowledge that social-support programs could contribute in any way to the causal factors underlying poverty. The general public may regard such positions as examples of political rhetoric, but that is no reason for ignoring the crucial question of exactly what the quantitative effects of such programs are, and for refusing to take these effects into account in selecting among alternative approaches to acknowledged social problems.

Acknowledging Social Statistics

Our highly individualistic social philosophy and our stress upon individual rights and responsibilities has made it very difficult for us to respond to, or even to recognize, problems which arise at the level of group organization. This is particularly so when the precise causal chain leading to personal loss (punishment) is only imperfectly understood. For example, suppose that we were to select groups of smokers and non-smokers from our own population in such a way that, apart from their smoking habits, the two groups were demographically and medically alike. It might even be convenient to separate the two groups geographically, establishing a city called Argos for the nonsmokers, and Troy for the smokers. Medical evidence which is widely available today indicates that if one were to measure the death rates in these two cities, one would find a higher rate in Troy; however, the immediate *causes* of death in the two cities would be drawn from the same set of diseases. Some persons in each city will be found to have died of complications arising from old age (although a relatively higher percent of these will be in Argos), some will have died of lung disease (relatively more of these in Troy), some will have died of heart disease (again, predominantly in Troy), and so on, but there are no diseases which are found exclusively in either Argos or Troy. Now, suppose that we planned to go to court to prosecute the manufacturers of cigarettes for selling a dangerously toxic product to the citizens of Troy. With the death of which particular citizen do we confront them? Since all the diseases which are found in Troy are also found in Argos it is impossible to prove that any one smoker would not have died in any case and of the same disease even if he had never smoked. This is so despite the fact that with its higher death rate, several hundred people a year may be dying in Troy who would not have died at the same age had they been nonsmoking residents of Argos. The problem, of course, is that cigarette smoking contributes to disease in a way which is not well enough understood for it to constitute a basis for a claim for damages in a court of law despite overwhelming statistical evidence that indicates the contribution is real and significant. So far as our legal system is concerned, the causal link is so attenuated that it can only be concluded that the injury is due to the disease and not to the smoking.

Given the formal structure which characterizes contemporary principles of law, it is understandable that the indirectness of statistical evidence is less than sufficient to sustain a legal action for personal injuries. Unfortunately, this problem seems to extend as well to legislative activities in which a bias against statistical data is far less defensible. How else are we to understand how a legislative body which imposes all sorts of safety standards and regulations upon automobiles, such as seat belt requirements or crash tolerance limits, can at the same time provide regular cash subsidies to tobacco growers? Evidently, one can use dummies and simulated crashes to demonstrate with a convincing immediacy that seat belts reduce the frequency and severity of personal injury and save lives, but no comparably graphic demonstrations exist which can make the dangers of cigarette smoking equally compelling. The statistical evidence of injury, however convincing it may be to scientists and doctors, is simply not yet acceptable to the people who put our social policies into place. In effect, our public officials are in the same traps which mislead private individuals when they carry out their own affairs. The separation of cause from effect has made it possible to ignore the connection, and, in this case, to behave as though the trap did not exist.

Rationality

In spite of our frequent failure to recognize the capacity of the legal system to produce far-reaching effects upon behavior, we have evolved a number of laws and procedures which presume that people make choices guided wholly by rationality. Whenever people are free to make choices, there is a strong presumption in the law that they should be held accountable for any consequences of those choices whatever the circumstances may be. This view of criminal behavior implies a model of law breaking in which the miscreant is seen as evaluating cost-benefit ratios for contemplated criminal acts in order to choose the optimal behavioral path. Under such an assumption, it is reasonable to suppose that increases in the "costs" would deter a crime. This is just what we attempt to do when we propose increases in the severity of criminal sanctions as means for reducing lawlessness. In effect, we deal with criminals as rational people who make free choices and who deserve whatever punishments are meted out to them. If choices were governed by rules of rationality, such deterrents might work: perfectly rational individuals could successfully bridge time delays, and they would be effective in implementing the kind of actuarial computations necessary to take intelligent account of the risk of punishment. In practice, however, there is a notable absence of rationality in much of the conduct which brings persons before the courts. Moreover, criminal sanctions are applied in a manner which greatly weakens any deterrent effect they might have. Criminal penalties are imposed only after very long delays, and even then their imposition is subject to considerable uncertainty.

When a suspect is captured, is released on bond, and then is discovered again engaging in the same crime, we have evidence that the time-delay problem is not being successfully solved. The impact of uncertainty is even more dramatic. The crime chieftain who has never spent a day in jail is widely regarded by the media and the general public as a successful criminal, not merely a lucky one. What we see as the uncertainty of punishment is perceived by others as the difference between the talented and the untalented. The criminal who has not yet been caught is more likely to take pride in that proof of his ability than he is to worry about the likelihood that eventually he, too, will be caught.

A similar problem arises if we return to our attempt to charge cigarette manufacturers for poisoning the citizens of Troy. All available information on the hazards of smoking is by now widely disseminated to the public, even to the extent of printing warnings on cigarette packages. If someone chooses to ignore this evidence, the manufacturer cannot be held responsible. Legal doctrines of "assumption of risk" and "contributory negligence" provide cigarette manufacturers with a defense against suits brought by cigarette-smoking plaintiffs. The tobacco industry can point to the warnings upon cigarette packs as proof that the plaintiff was duly warned of the dangers of smoking. Having been warned, it is presumed that the decision to smoke was rational and voluntary, a measured acceptance of the risks in fair exchange for the pleasures of smoking. Therefore, the rationality assumption implicit in our legal theories may be used in defense against a suit brought by one who suffered a detriment from behaving nonrationally.

On the legislative side, we have a similar tendency to accept the proposition that "choice" is always "rational choice." The decision to raise money through state lotteries is a good example of such a bias. If we believe that all gamblers are acting upon the basis of rational principles, and that they are buying tickets which pay back at most fifty cents on the dollar because of the excitement which the lottery provides, then these states are providing a useful service by making such ready recreation possible. If the average citizen buys lottery tickets because he or she is a below average actuary, or if intermittent reinforcement is the powerful influence that experimentation shows it to be, then these states are exploiting their own citizens by driving them farther into a trap.

Externality Traps and Civil Law

Obviously, the victim of an externality trap should sue. If the air pollution from Peter's cement plant, his loud Beethoven recordings, or his slow driving on crowded highways are offensive to us, we naturally consider the legal system as providing a possible source of protection under the law of "torts": an area of law which deals with the conflicts which arise when one party claims to have suffered from the action, negligence, or trespass of another. Two questions are of concern to us here. First, how effective is the legal system in providing relief when injury results from externality traps? Second, if the courts do provide protection in this first sense, will that be of a nature sufficient to eliminate externality traps?

We have repeatedly advocated the use of devices which make reinforcer trade-offs explicit as means for avoiding or escaping from traps. In the case of externality traps, this amounts to confronting individuals with the full consequences of their actions. By means of monetary or other devices, we would charge Peter for the harm he does to others so that the reinforcers which shape his behavior can match more closely the values and needs of the society as a whole. In principle, one might consider our legal system to be an ideal vehicle for accomplishing this end, and it is unfortunate that, for practical reasons, most of us would dismiss the law as a potential source of relief without giving the matter much thought. Even a brief consideration of the many impediments to the efficient implementation of legal procedures demonstrates that as presently constituted, they can be effective in only the most straightforward cases. Even when used, our contemporary principles of law are frequently incompatible with our objective—the trade-offs which are imposed by law may be as badly distorted as those which were responsible for the original trap. Several of the most prevalent difficulties encountered when resorting to legal remedies are found in the following:

A. An action in tort provides only a limited range of relief to the plaintiff: either monetary payment in an amount commensurate with the injury suffered, or, alternatively, "injunctive relief." The principle of monetary relief comes close to our suggestion of replacing individual reinforcers with social ones, and it is in this setting that legal remedies may be efficacious in resolving traps. Injunctive relief, on the other hand, introduces no trade-off at all, but simply forbids the activity. In effect, it permits the party who is harmed to prevent someone else from engaging in profitable behavior. The trap is reversed, and it is the plaintiff who, by failing to respond to the benefits of the activity, imposes a loss upon others. Depending upon how large the total benefits and losses are, an injunction may be better than the original trap, but neither solution is better than one in which Peter is taxed for any damage which he does, so that the decision whether or not to engage in the activity, and to what extent, is made in direct response to social payoffs.

B. Supposing that we wish to make use of the monetary remedy which is made available through legal action, the high cost of using the system is itself a hindrance. In order to succeed in a legal action intended to shift a loss back to its source, the complaining party must meet an impressive list of demands: he must show that a legal obligation is owed to him, that the obligation has been breached, that some harm or injury has been suffered as a consequence of the breach, and that the party responsible for causing the harm has been correctly identified. Even if the complaining party successfully meets these requirements, he must overcome the other defenses which the defending party will almost certainly raise, he must wait out the long delays imposed by crowded court dockets, and finally he must pay his own attorneys. Even then the outcome is uncertain, however well-prepared, expensive, and justified the legal action may have been. To an extent, the high costs of legal action may be offset by the contingent-fee method of payment for legal services, but such a fee system still reduces the level of compensation available to the plaintiff. Furthermore, it has the potential of producing conflicts of interest between client and attorney if they appraise the likelihood of success differently. It might be simpler and more efficacious for the plaintiff simply to punch the defendant in the nose, but however well deserved, even this behavior is likely to be inhibited by the fear of a lawsuit.

C. Many externality traps are of a type which are not amenable to any orthodox legal remedy. Examples of the inadequacy of conventional remedies abound in the legal doctrines surrounding the tort law dealing with "nuisance." Nuisance in law refers to situations in which the activities of one party interfere with another party's "use and enjoyment" of property where such interference occurs without physical trespass, i.e., actual entry upon the property of the injured party. This distinction between nuisance and trespass has itself taken up much time and effort on the part of the courts because before any action can be taken, one must settle technical questions concerning what constitutes a physical invasion; that is, do sonic booms, beams of light, dust particles, or offensive odors constitute direct or indirect physical intrusion? Moreover, once it is established that the nuisance interpretation is appropriate, the plaintiff must still show that the defendant party is carrying out an unacceptable or unreasonable activity, that this activity intrudes upon the use and enjoyment of property, and that the intrusion has resulted in damage, loss, or reduction in the value of the plaintiff's property. Many everyday nuisances fail to meet some or all of these tests. For example, aesthetic enjoyment is regarded by the courts as so subjective in nature as to defy easy definition. Therefore, courts have generally refused to allow nuisance suits to succeed where the loss suffered is intangible and not easily quantifiable into monetary terms. However obvious it may be that a homeowner suffers when a neighbor paints his house chartreuse, the courts, wary of fraudulent or exaggerated claims for damages and unwilling to act as mediators or arbitrators of subjective values, will allow a damage claim only if evidence of monetary loss can be shown. (Of course, one might hire real estate agents who will testify as to the loss of market value which has been suffered, but the defendant is equally at liberty to find his own witnesses who consider chartreuse to be a lovely color and an asset to any neighborhood.) The same problems apply to other forms of subjective damage. Generally, a claim for pain, suffering, or other purely psychological distress will not be sufficiently "objective" and measurable to allow the award of damages to the plaintiff. Thus rock-music fans who drive their Bach-loving neighbors to move away, snowmobilers who disrupt our enjoyment of placid winter scenes, and dawdling drivers who reduce the availability of our pleasurable hours on the beach are all generating externalities, but their activities are well within legal limits.

D. When an activity carried out by one party produces undesirable consequences which are so widespread as to affect an entire community, the nuisance is said to be "public." The significance of this legal distinction rests in the fact that only public officials may initiate action to stop a public nuisance. Further, the courts restrict the remedy in public-nuisance cases to injunctions. They may order the nuisance-generating activity to cease but will not impose monetary penalties. Thus the law allows the anomalous result that if the number of persons who suffer loss and discomfort is sufficiently large, the one who produces those consequences is not required (or given the opportunity) to pay for them. In this instance it is impossible to introduce trap-avoiding trade-offs, and the only remaining remedy is trap reversal in which public officials put a stop to the activity, however beneficial it may be to those who would like to carry it out.

E. Another doctrine which poses barriers to the effective application of contemporary law to traps is the old principle of *de minimis* damages or injuries, which was designed to keep trivial or insignificant issues from taking up the time of the courts; if the alleged loss or injury were "small," the principle could be used to dismiss the action. Thus if the injury to any one member of the public is slight, the *de minimis* principle can be invoked to bar legal action, even though millions of people may be affected in that same (slight) way, magnifying the damage into something quite substantial.

Another aspect of the *de minimis* doctrine which causes problems in dealing with externality traps is that in many circumstances the contribution of harm made by any one individual is so trivially small as to preclude legal intervention. If the number of people who do small amounts of harm is extremely large, and if their contributions are additive, a serious externality trap can be created. The amount of fluorocarbons released into the atmosphere by one deodorant spray is insignificant. Yet millions of spraying citizens can alter the earth's atmosphere and increase the incidence of skin cancer. It is difficult to deal with this type of situation because the legal system traditionally requires well-defined "parties of interest" before intervention by the courts. To a certain extent, the invention and elaboration of the plaintiff class-action suit provides some answer to the problem of a large plaintiff or "injured" group. However, no corresponding class action theory has been developed to deal with a large group of *defendants*. A smoke-filled room may be annoying to us or possibly even damaging to our health, but we cannot bring any one individual smoker to court to enjoin the harm he might be doing, since it is trivially small, and we cannot bring the entire group of smokers in as a defendant class, because the necessary legal framework does not even exist.

F. Suppose that a polluting activity currently underway is sought to be enjoined because of its prospective harmful consequences. A typical judicial basis for nonintervention would be that the future harm is too remote, too speculative, and too uncertain in its effects to justify an interruption of production, job layoffs, or the expense of pollution-abatement machinery. In effect, this denies standing to future generations (or even to ourselves a few years from now), in any action to prevent current activities from doing harm to future well-being. A striking example of such judicial reluctance is found in the litigation which has accompanied attempts to prevent the dumping of asbestos fiber–laden taconite into Lake Superior. Although these asbestos fibers have already entered the drinking water supplies of nearby communities, the courts have held that preventing the danger of future harm to the health of the communities would be more than offset by the immediate economic disruption which an injunction would produce. Indeed, some workers and others who benefit economically from the presence of the mining operations have expressed their own willingness to undertake the risk of future disease and continue mining operations. Thus there remains no mechanism even to evaluate the possibility that we have entered into a time-delay trap in which we sacrifice the well-being of our descendants for the sake of current gratification.

Compensations and Trade-offs

In a law suit familiar to environmental attorneys, *Boomer v. Atlantic Cement Co.*, a New York court was faced with a typical nuisance situation. A large cement-manufacturing company, located in the vicinity of private homes, was imposing property damage upon the nearby homeowners. A group of them brought suit against the cement company to recover damages they had suffered and to enjoin future production activities at the plant. In refusing to issue the injunction, the court spoke of the economic disruptions which a shutdown would cause and of the necessity to maintain a favorable climate for business. However, in a significant departure from traditional legal remedies, the court devised a new approach to the externality situation. In effect the company was required to pay the homeowners for those damages which they had already sustained, and in addition, for damages which were *anticipated* if production were allowed to continue. This additional compensation constituted a novel legal strategy which eliminated the externality trap by granting the cement company the option of continuing their production only if they were willing to pay a greater portion of the true costs of production. This judgment suffered from some of the deficiencies outlined in the preceding paragraphs, particularly in that it restricted compensable damages only to what could be reflected in decreased property values; nevertheless, it represented a significant advance in the direction of judicially imposing trade-off elements into externality traps.

It is crucial to the understanding of the trade-off device that one recognize that from a behavioral point of view it is irrelevant whether or not the monetary punishment imposed upon the Atlantic Cement Company actually was paid as compensation to the plaintiffs. If what we seek is to induce the company to behave in a way which reflects the total costs and benefits accrued to society, then the imposition of the penalty is sufficient. That the plaintiffs should receive the award (or what was left of it after legal expenses) may appeal to our sense of fairness, but that is incidental to the behavioral question and its solution. Moreover, the fact that plaintiffs do so often receive compensation in civil cases introduces some very difficult new traps.

In the *Boomer v. Atlantic Cement Co.* case, compensation was paid only to the specific plaintiffs who brought the suit. Any newcomer who chose to build a house in the same area would not be eligible for compensation because the presence of the nuisance would by then be well known, and a court will generally not grant the claim of a plaintiff who is found to have "come to the nuisance." On this principle, compensation would be denied to anyone who had the capacity to avoid the nuisance in the first place. Thus compensation would not be granted to someone who built a rest home next door to a foundry, or to a temperance group which rented an office over a tavern. This principle is usually appropriate, for it is clear that its abandonment would reverse the trap rather than undo it. If anyone who chose to live in the neighborhood of the cement company were fully compensated for the externality from which he suffered, there would be no reason to avoid new housing construction in that location, and the costs imposed upon the company would be magnified by the presence of those who could as easily have chosen to live elsewhere. The penalties suffered by the firm then would become unnecessarily high, and what was determined before to be a beneficial activity on balance might be forced to cease. The point is that in giving a business an incentive to avoid imposing costs upon others, we do not wish to remove from those others the incentive to avoid being the targets of the losses. If anyone who lived in the vicinity of an airport could successfully sue for compensation because of the noise, there would be no reason for home builders to avoid the area, and the cost of operating the airport might become so high as to render it economically infeasible, in spite of the fact that the home building could, with little loss, have been carried out elsewhere.

On the other hand, suppose that the general area has become so crowded that there are virtually no places to build other than the vicinities of the cement plant or the airport. Then, even though the people have "come to the nuisance," the cement plant and airport are imposing additional external costs, and the efficient trade-off principle requires that they face up to these higher costs. Those payments, however, still should not be given to the newcomers. One must bear in mind that the victims of externality traps also behave in ways which are responsive to the reinforcers which surround them, and compensation potentially directs behavior into traps. This fact is already familiar to insurance companies who recognize that when they contract to compensate victims of accidents, they reduce people's incentives to avoid those accidents. From a policy holder's point of view, insurance against fire or theft is in part a substitute for household security and alarm systems. Insurance companies have learned that they must take account of a slackening of concern on the part of the insured when they calculate actuarial values for expected insurance losses. Exactly the same problem arises if we propose compensation in externality traps in which some people have discretionary control over their vulnerability to the punishments induced by others' behavior. Thus an ideal trap-avoiding law would penalize individuals for the harm which they do to others. In addition, it would give premiums to those who convey indirect benefits to others, but it would not pay compensation or impose taxes upon those who suffer or benefit from the behavior, unless it was clear that those payments or taxes would not serve as reinforcers which could bait new traps. From a behavioral point of view, it is irrelevant whether or not we compensate those whose houses were in place before the cement company commenced operations, but to compensate newcomers would be to invite entry into a new trap.

In our interpretation, trap avoidance is a social responsibility that requires a special sort of social legislation which is more akin to our criminal law than it is to our civil law. Since both are forms of social control, it is curious that these two bodies of law are so different in their emphases. By focusing upon an individual's right to compensation and upon the amount of damage suffered, civil actions ignore the incentives which confront the parties, perhaps on the unfounded assumption that what is the "right" compensation for the plaintiff must provide everyone with the "right" incentives. Criminal law, on the other hand, focuses upon the use of punishment as a means for influencing the behavior of defendants, both actual and potential, while ignoring entirely the possibility of providing compensation to victims. There are now a few states which have instituted programs of compensation for victims of crime, but funds for this purpose come from public revenues, and the sums which are paid out are trivial compared to those which would be awarded under civil law. In any case, support for these victim compensation programs may stem from a desire to confront legislators with more accurate social reinforcers. Since state and local budgets support crime prevention and detention activities but do not ordinarily pay for the personal losses brought about by crime, there may be a tendency in times of stringency for legislatures to fall into the trap of reducing crime-control activities, thus shifting the cost of (potential) crime out of the budget and onto the general public. Compensation for the victims of crime may replace this trap with a trade-off within the legislative budget itself.

It may seem harsh to deny compensation to those who suffer from the externality-producing behavior of others, but one must bear in mind that there are often other sources of relief which offset these losses. Land in the vicinity of airports is usually cheaper than land elsewhere; the externality through market forces leads quite naturally to lower living costs, and residents who choose to live there are to that extent better off.

A legal approach to the solution of traps which does not stress compensation has a further advantage in that it reduces the incentive to bring fraudulent or exaggerated claims of damage because the plaintiffs do not stand to gain direct financial rewards from their suit. It is the avoidance of these distortions and exaggerations of losses which makes the injunction remedy attractive to courts faced with suits arising from externality traps. However, as we have already noted, injunctions are of no use in introducing constructive trade-off elements into traps, and for this reason, procedures which did impose quantitative damages but did not award "prizes" to the winners would be much superior.

Public Goods

Externality traps can appear in two versions that might be described as positive and negative forms of the trap. In the negative version someone engages in a behavior which is rewarded, but which causes or imposes a loss upon others. In the positive version a person fails to act in a manner which would benefit others because they obtain insufficient rewards for themselves by doing so. If Peter buys a soft drink and throws the empty bottle onto the street, his littering is an example of a negative trap. If Pamela comes along on her bicycle and fails to pick up the bottle, the trap continues, this time in its positive form because a behavior which might have had external benefits is insufficiently reinforced. This trap might be avoided by rewarding picking-up activities as well as by punishing littering activities, and in fact, by 1979, a few states such as Michigan, Oregon, and Vermont had enacted legislation intended to do just that. By imposing deposit charges for bottles and cans and then refunding these deposits when the empties are returned, these laws impose socially efficient trade-offs which will work to inhibit Peter's littering and, failing that, encourage Pamela to pick up the empties. In effect, a bounty is placed upon empty bottles, and if Peter does not wish to collect it someone else presumably will.

Unfortunately, there seems to be a widespread attitude that if a behavior has external benefits, then attempts to encourage that behavior should be funded by charges levied against only the beneficiaries of that behavior. However reasonable this view may appear at first glance, it creates a trap which is an exact counterpart of that which arises when compensation is paid to the victims of a negative externality. If we tax the beneficiaries who gain from a positive externality, we reduce the incentive for them to behave in ways that gain the benefits, and a potential good is lost. Suppose that a museum is to be built in Argos County, and that it is proposed to pay for the museum by levying property taxes solely upon the residents of that county. The high tax cost of the museum may so offset its benefits that Argos County is no more attractive a place to live than it was before, and potential residents who would have benefitted from proximity to the museum fail to move in. Suppose instead that the cost of the museum is spread over the

entire nation. Then the attractiveness of Argos County is greatly increased, and many more people move there. In this case,
the social benefits of the museum are much greater because
now more persons are served by it. This is not just a question
of nonresidents paying for some benefits to residents, although that certainly happens. Aggregate social welfare has
increased because the museum serves many more people at no
increased cost. Moreover, the redistributive problem may be
only temporary, as a larger population of Argos County may
eventually be able to support the museum without any support from outside.

There is a danger that even when we recognize positive
externality traps, our desire to have only direct beneficiaries
pay to establish trap-avoiding trade-offs has greatly reduced
the effectiveness of the trade-offs which we devise. Indeed,
many potentially beneficial remedial programs may have been
eliminated entirely. An example of the problems that this attitude can generate is provided by the "bottle-bill" legislation.
The Michigan bottle law, for example, applies only to bottles
bought in that state. In effect, Peter has been given an incentive to buy his soft drinks out of state where they are cheaper
since no deposit is charged, and then to continue to throw his
bottles away as before. Pamela has no incentive to pick up
out-of-state bottles, for no bounty is attached to them, and so
at least some litter problem remains. Moreover, the deposit-
return device has introduced enormous sorting costs upon
grocery stores (and therefore consumers) which now must
separate and store empties for each beer and soft drink sup-
plier, despite the fact that from a resource standpoint it is
irrelevant who originally produced each container. The flaw in
the enacted bottle bills is that the return of bottles is treated as
the responsibility of individual purchasers who should pay to
have bottles returned, rather than as a trap-avoiding social
responsibility. If the state were simply to fund ecology centers
to pay five to ten cents each for any Michigan-sold bottle or
can, and the centers resold those (reuseable) bottles and (recy-
clable) cans, there would be no incentive for people to buy soft

drinks elsewhere, the economic costs of the program would be much lower, and the welfare benefits would be much higher.

Contracts

In requiring the Atlantic Cement Company to pay compensation to surrounding homeowners, the court was in effect imposing a contract upon the parties under which the company was to "buy" from the homeowners the right to continue its operations. In principle, any externality trap could be resolved through the device of voluntary contracting. If we dislike Peter's chartreuse house in our neighborhood, we could buy a different color from him by writing a contract under which, for a sum of money, he agrees to paint his house a more acceptable color. If the damages caused by the Atlantic Cement Company were intolerable, the surrounding homeowners could have contracted with the company to have pollution control equipment installed, to schedule its production during certain hours or seasons, or even to move away, and as a result, property values would rise and possibly compensate the homeowners for the cost of the contract.

Many potential externality traps are in fact handled in this way. For hundreds of years, restrictions concerning land use have been written into property deeds; the purchase of a building lot with restrictions as to commercial use, set-backs from property lines, or building size amount to sales of certain rights to someone else. That potential traps are thereby avoided is clear: if only one deed in a large community permitted commercial uses, while the others did not, that one piece of property would be more valuable. But, if none of the deeds had such restrictions, the "stability" of the community would be in question, and all the property might be worth less.

An astonishing fact which was first detailed by Ronald Coase in 1960 is that the efficacy of the contracting device in avoiding traps is unaffected by the distribution of "rights" which may be determined under civil law. If Peter has the "right" to paint his house chartreuse, then we must contract to pay him if we wish the house to be white. If we have the right to enjoin Peter from painting his house chartreuse, then *he* would have to pay *us* through a contract if he wished to use that color. The color which is finally chosen, however, is unaffected by these alternatives. To make the matter concrete, suppose that Peter's neighbors stand to suffer a collective loss of $1,000 if Peter paints his house chartreuse, while Peter himself is so enamored of that color that the house would thereby be made $900 more valuable to him. If Peter has the right to choose his color, the neighbors could contract to pay him $950 to use white instead: they gain $50, Peter himself is also $50 better off, and since the house is now white, the trap is avoided. If the neighbors had the right to enjoin Peter from using chartreuse, he would be willing to pay no more than $900 to them to allow him to do so. This offer would be refused, and again the house would be white. In either case, the trap is avoided, although clearly Peter is better off in the first case than he is in the second.

Suppose that instead of $900, Peter valued a chartreuse house at $1,100. Then the neighbors would not pay him enough to get him to agree to white because that is only worth $1,000 to them. If they had the power to enjoin Peter from using chartreuse, he could offer to pay them $1,050 for the right to do so, and this contract would be accepted. Again, the trap would be avoided, this time with a chartreuse house, although as before, Peter's general welfare is higher if he has the right to choose his own color in the first place. Coase's conclusion is that while the distribution of individual welfare is certainly influenced by the distribution of rights under civil law, the trap-avoiding outcomes which can be effected through voluntary contracting are not. (This conclusion is generally modified through an observation that if Peter's valuation of a chartreuse house depends upon how rich he is, then the distribution of ownership of rights may influence the outcome, but this problem is usually seen to be of secondary importance.)

The question arises as to why contracts are not more widely used for the purpose of resolving externality traps. There are certainly many arguments in their favor: contracts are much cheaper to use than are court proceedings; they are more reliable in their effects; they are not confined to any particular form of externality, but can be applied to aesthetic as well as monetary damages; and they involve only persons directly concerned with the transaction, rather than appealing to the judgments of third parties who may be quite unfamiliar with the entire problem.

Some externality traps are resistant to the informal contract solution because potential parties to the contract may not feel bound to negotiate at all. In many circumstances, one may obtain certain benefits "for free," while avoiding any obligations to offset the negative externalities which these gains impose upon others. This can sometimes be accomplished because the person creating the externalities can do so anonymously. One cannot forecast whose truck it will be that impedes traffic on the way to beach or what litterbug is going to be responsible for all the bottles and cans along the roadway. The anonymity may even be deliberate: some people go out of their way to leave empty beer cans in remote and secluded places; factories discharge their pollutants into rivers at night; and oil tankers pump out their bilge on the open sea, outside the territorial waters of affected countries. It would be naive to expect that negative externality-causing parties would voluntarily contract to pay for the imposition of harm upon others if they can do so without detection.

Another difficulty with the voluntary contract approach as a solution to externality traps is that a proliferation of externality-induced contracts would increase the complexity of property transactions enormously. The cost of an individual contract may be low, but the cost of investigating ownership of property which may be encumbered by a variety of agreements might be so high as to offset the benefits of the original trap-avoidance devices. Still another problem is that though the behavior which avoids traps may be independent of the allocation of rights under civil law, the actual form of the contract which must be written is not. Questions arise concerning which party would be required to make payments to the other, and resolution of this issue would be subject to all of the legal problems described earlier.

The most important objection to the use of contracts comes from the fact that, like other aspects of civil law, contracts introduce a system of compensatory payments, and these compensations can have behavioral effects upon those who receive them, introducing new traps just as one is led out of old ones. To illustrate this problem, let us suppose that our cement plant is surrounded by a mixture of private residences and vacant land. We have already argued that the cement plant could be directed into socially appropriate behavior if it is made to pay for any pollution damage which it imposes upon homeowners. If homeowners have the legal right to enjoin polluting activities, then the company must negotiate a contract with them to pay them to have the privilege of continuing to pollute. But what of the owners of the vacant land also subject to pollution by the plant? Since no one wants to buy such land, its market value is certainly below the value of unaffected land located elsewhere. At the same time, the cement plant imposes no ongoing physical damage upon the vacant land, and if the land has been owned for so long that the effects of inflation or inheritance have removed any suggestion of financial loss, then the owners have no grounds upon which to base any demand for contractual payments from the company to reflect the damage to land value.

Owners of land do have the right to develop their properties as they choose, however, and this often includes the right to build residences. Since residences are demonstrably affected by the presence of the cement plant, the landowners could build and thus acquire the right to compensatory payments. In short, the property owners must either build where it makes no sense to build, or they must *threaten* to build and induce the company to contract with them not to do so (possibly by buying the land outright at prices comparable to prices of building lots which are unaffected by the pollution). The first of these alternatives creates a new trap by having houses built in inappropriate locations, and the second has much of the character of blackmail. The outcome then is that either the company pays too large a price for its operations because it pays for damages to houses which should never have been built, or it pays too low a price because there are no legal grounds on which owners of vacant land can impose costs for the damage done to them.

Trap Law

We can summarize our discussion by reviewing what sort of changes in our current legal system and in our legislative attitudes are called for if legal remedies are to be effectively applied to social traps. First, and most crucially, there must be greater awareness upon the part of both the courts and legislators that their decisions do not merely allocate rights and privileges among the individuals presently before them, but that they shape behavior to come. Every decision as to who is in the right, who is in the wrong, who is to be punished, and who is to receive rewards is indirectly a decision as to how many people in the future will be acting so as to receive those rights and rewards, and how many will be acting so as to avoid the punishments. Changes in the rules change behavior, and when legislatures promulgate new laws or courts articulate new precedents, they do so most effectively if they take account of the new social incentives which they are creating.

Second, it is time to acknowledge that while behavior is shaped by circumstances, there is no guarantee that the behavior which emerges will be consonant with the interests of either the individual or society. Delays in time and the uncertainty of outcome not only reduce the influence upon behavior of rewards and punishments; they place the entire learning-reinforcement mechanism into an arena in which clear rationality is rarely encountered. To assume that the cigarette smoker, the gambler, or the alcoholic driver are responding in their own self-interest to overall payoff schedules is to ignore much of what is known about the psychological determinants of behavior. To write laws which protect and encourage tobacco growers, which offer citizens gambling opportunities through state lotteries, or which simply fine drinking drivers is to put government on the wrong side—with the trap rather than against it.

Third, it is time to take group statistical data more seriously when formulating social policy. While it is true that there are a multitude of ways to interpret statistics, that fact should not provide an excuse for ignoring data altogether. We are still prone to gather our information by placing reliance upon self-interested advocates of specific causes and upon selected case histories which serve only to illustrate a particular point of view. We would serve ourselves better if we were to look to widely gathered, broad-based social statistics before formulating laws and setting legal precedents. It is the abstraction and generality of social data which makes it a potentially useful source of information. Unfortunately, it is the very generality and abstraction of statistical data which seems to put us off and cause us to rely instead upon the more personalistic and all too often more persuasive arguments of spokespersons with vested interests.

Fourth, it is time to review the efficacy of traditional civil court procedures in dealing with externality traps. It must be recognized that in our modern world, whose technology dictates that the fates of so many people be tied together, the solutions of our problems are found in a measured restructuring of incentives rather than in administrative attempts to redirect behavior by fiat. Injunctive remedies almost never resolve traps because they never permit the quantitative adjustment to divergent interests that trap-avoidance usually requires. Other limitations of civil law actions which are equally destructive are that attention is given only to those parties before the court; that courts are reluctant to deal with injuries or losses that are probabilistic in nature or remote in time; and that courts are generally unwilling to impose affirmative obligations or duties upon persons to respect the rights and interests of others. Traditional legal doctrines such as *de minimis* loss, burdens of proof, duty of care, and proximate cause must be reexamined as well. Finally, we must replace the pervasive emphasis upon the compensation of victims with analyses of the reinforcement schedules which create victims in the first place.

Legislative attempts to resolve traps are too often hampered by the fact that members of a legislative body may become enmeshed in traps as part of their law-generating activities. A legislator is motivated to write wise law, but he must also manage to get reelected. Obviously, these two goals are not always compatible; when wise law calls for long-range planning at the expense of short-term interests, elected officials find themselves in institutionalized time-delay traps. In effect, the system forces them to make decisions which cater to short-term interests at the expense of the long run. Unfortunately, the trap does not affect legislators alone. The entire society is drawn into the trap with them. In this sense, our legal system is subject to many of the same divergent pressures that generate defective individual behaviors. Just as various means must be found to explicate the mechanisms and reinforcement contingencies which get individuals and groups into traps, attention must be directed to our social institutions to understand the traps to which they are subject.

In our view, effective legal mechanisms for dealing with externality traps would have more in common with criminal law than with existing civil law. It would involve a judicial and legislative approach in which the emphasis would be upon redirecting individual behavior rather than upon mechanisms for compensating victims. Trap law would depart from criminal law in some important respects, however. It would place equal emphasis upon countertraps, and there would be legislative efforts to provide incentives for those behaviors which produce widespread benefits, without confining them to those systems in which only potential benefactors pay the cost.

Even in the case of severe negative externality traps, we certainly would wish legal remedies to avoid the sort of social opprobrium which is the fate of those who get caught up in the criminal justice system. A major purpose of this book has been to challenge the easy notion that somewhere one can find "guilty" parties who are responsible for social problems and who could then be prosecuted and punished as common criminals. Traps come about, not because someone has broken a law (even a moral law), but because persons behave in ways which have been guided by the reinforcing circumstances of their lives. The very behavioral means which ensure our survival as a species—the ability to learn, to adapt to changing environment, and to modify our actions so as to gain rewards and avoid pain—sometimes go awry. When that happens we are betrayed by our own instincts and find ourselves reaching destinations remote from our best interests. We must come to understand that our maps are sometimes poor and our compasses faulty, and we should be able to recognize that some directions are bad directions without attributing evil intentions to those who lose their way.

Bibliography

Bator, F. M. "The Anatomy of Market Failure." *Quarterly Journal of Economics*, August 1958, pp. 351–79.

Berne, E. *Games People Play*. New York: Grove Press, 1964.

Buchanan, J. M. "An Economic Theory of Clubs." *Economica*, February 1965, pp. 1–14.

Chamberlin, E. H. *The Theory of Monopolistic Competition*. 6th ed. Cambridge, Mass.: Harvard University Press, 1950.

Clarke, E. H. "Multipart Pricing of Public Goods." *Public Choice* 11 (1971):17–33.

Coase, R. "The Problem of Social Cost." *Journal of Law and Economics*, October 1960, pp. 1–44.

Cournot, A. *Researches into the Mathematical Principles of the Theory of Wealth*. New York: Macmillan, 1897.

Cross, J. G. "A Stochastic Learning Model of Economic Behavior." *Quarterly Journal of Economics*, May 1973, pp. 239–66.

Ferster, C., and Skinner, B. F. *Schedules of Reinforcement*. New York: Appleton-Century-Crofts, 1957.

Fisher, I. *The Theory of Interest*. Augustus M. Kelly Reprint, 1961.

Groves, T. "Incentives in Teams." *Econometrica* 45 (1977):617–63.

Groves, T., and Ledyard, J. "Optimal Allocation of Public Goods: A Solution to the 'Free Rider' Problem." *Econometrica* 45 (1977): 783–809.

Hamburger, H. *Games as Models of Social Phenomena*. San Francisco: W. H. Freeman and Co., 1979.

Hardin, G. "The Tragedy of the Commons." *Science* 162 (1968): 1243–48.

Hilgard, E. R., and Bower, G. H. *Theories of Learning*. New York: Appleton-Century-Crofts, 1968.

Honig, W. K., ed. *Operant Behavior: Areas of Research and Application*. New York: Appleton-Century-Crofts, 1966.

Kimble, G. A. "Conditioning as a Function of the Time between Conditioned and Unconditioned Stimuli." *Journal of Experimental Psychology* 37 (1947):1–15.

Luce, R. D., and Raiffa, H. *Games and Decisions: Introduction and Critical Survey*. New York: Wiley, 1957.

Rapoport, A.; Guyer, M.; and Gordon, D. *The 2 × 2 Game*. Ann Arbor: University of Michigan Press, 1976.

Samuelson, P. "The Pure Theory of Public Expenditures." *Review of Economics and Statistics* 36 (1954):387–89.

Schelling, T. C. *The Strategy of Conflict*. Cambridge, Mass.: Harvard University Press, 1960.

Schelling, T. "The Ecology of Micromotives." *Public Interest* 25 (1971): 61–98.

Scitovsky, T. *The Joyless Economy*. New York: Oxford University Press, 1976.

Shubik, M. "The Dollar Auction Game: A Paradox in Noncooperative Behavior and Escalation." *Journal of Conflict Resolution* 15 (1971): 109–11.

Sidowski, J. B.; Wykoff, L. B.; and Tabory, H. "The Influence of Reinforcement and Punishment in a Minimal Social Situation." *Journal of Abnormal and Social Psychology* 52 (1956):115–19.

Simon, H. A. "A Comparison of Game Theory and Learning Theory." *Psychometrika* 21 (1956):267–72.

Skinner, B. F. *Beyond Freedom and Dignity*. New York: Alfred A. Knopf, 1971.

———. *Contingencies of Reinforcement: A Theoretical Analysis*. New York: Appleton-Century-Crofts, 1969.

———. "Superstition in the Pigeon," *Journal of Experimental Psychology* 38 (1948):168–72.

Suppes, P., and Atkinson, R. C. *Markov Learning Models for Multiperson Interaction*. Stanford: Stanford University Press, 1960.

Truax, C. B. "Reinforcement and Non-reinforcement in Rogerian Psychotherapy." *Journal of Abnormal and Social Psychology* 11 (1966): 1–9.

Vickery, W. "Counterspeculation, Auctions, and Competitive Sealed Tenders." *Journal of Finance,* March 1961, pp. 8–37.

Von Neumann, J., and Morgenstern, O. *The Theory of Games and Economic Behavior.* Princeton: Princeton University Press, 1947.

Whaley, D. L., and Malott, R. W. *Elementary Principles of Behavior.* Behaviordelia, 1968.

Williams, C. D. "Case Report: Elimination of Tantrum Behavior by Extinction Procedures." *Journal of Abnormal and Social Psychology* 59 (1959):269.